Keynes's Uncertain Revolution

Keynes's
Uncertain Revolution

BRADLEY W. BATEMAN

Ann Arbor
THE UNIVERSITY OF MICHIGAN PRESS

Copyright © by Bradley W. Bateman 1996
All rights reserved
Published in the United States of America by
The University of Michigan Press
Manufactured in the United States of America
⊚ Printed on acid-free paper

1999 1998 1997 1996   4 3 2 1

A CIP catalog record for this book is available from the British Library.

Library of Congress Cataloging-in-Publication Data

Bateman, Bradley W., 1956–
    Keynes's uncertain revolution / Bradley W. Bateman.
        p.   cm.
    Includes bibliographical references and index.
    ISBN 0-472-10708-9 (hardcover : alk. paper)
    1. Keynes, John Maynard, 1883–1946—Views on uncertainty.
    2. Keynes, John Maynard, 1883–1946—Views on probabilities.
    I. Title.
    HB103.K47B333   1996
    330.15′6—dc20   96-14662
                                                                CIP

For my wife

The Good Life

We could plot it on paper as a simple protuberant curve
rising from left to right and falling again;
or state it, no doubt, as a formula, as x
relating to y, equalling nothing perhaps.
It is the shape of average and scatter, any smooth curve
or distribution, 'unimodal', as the term
has it, and expressing standard deviations from the mean.

These may be relevant things, but it also seems
that just that it can be plotted, that quantity,
the referent of space and time, is here
the referent also, enforcing them, is the good.
We don't resemble this. We learn to use
the wrong terms always to deal with our lives:
terms with nothing at all to do with us.

—William Bronk

Preface

When I first began to research Maynard Keynes's interest in probability and uncertainty in 1981, all the work on the topic was written by economists. Indeed, almost everything written about Keynes was by economists, for economists. The study of Keynes took place largely in an hermetically sealed world in which the main point of the exercise was to identify his work as the precursor to some contemporary theoretical development. Once his status as a precursor was established, he was either an important ally in the writer's cause or the object of contumely. There were, of course, exceptions to this rule—Sue Howson, Donald Winch, and Don Moggridge come to mind—but their exceptions proved the rule. And in the specific area of my interest, in 1981, there were *no* exceptions; the explications of Keynes's interest in probability and uncertainty always pointed to some contemporary development in economic theory. Indeed, the interest in Keynes's work on probability circa 1981 sprang largely from the then current "rational expectations revolution" and the full-tilt gallop to introduce expectations to macroeconomics.

During the time which I have worked on this project, however, the study of Keynes has changed dramatically. Economists no longer have a monopoly. Historians, political scientists, philosophers, and sociologists have all taken an interest in Keynes's life and work, and the biographies by Don Moggridge and Robert Skidelsky have helped to change the way we think about and situate Keynes. Thus, to be effective, an economist writing on Keynes must write a different kind of history than the ones produced 15 years ago.

Many people have helped me in trying to write a book which fits in this new milieu. This was not always their intention, of course, but all of these people met with, talked with, argued with, corresponded with, or put up with me during the years that I worked on this project: Roger Backhouse, Tom Baldwin, Ted Bromund, Anna Carabelli, Peter Clarke, Allin Cottrell, John Davis, Neil de Marchi, Mary Ann Dimand, Robert Dimand, Nicholas Dimsdale, Bill Ferguson, Richard

Gift, Donald Gillies, Geoff Harcourt, Abe Hirsch, Kevin Hoover, Susan Howson, Terence Hutchison, Mike Lawlor, Tony Lawson, James Meade, Don Moggridge, Mary Morgan, Rod O'Donnell, Margaret Paul, Jochen Runde, Margaret Schabas, Yuichi Shionoya, Don Smith, and Roy Weintraub. I thank all of these people for their time and patience; none of them is responsible for anything I have said.

I owe a special debt of gratitude to Jacky Cox. None of my archival work at King's College, Cambridge, would have been possible without her tireless, pleasant help. Peter Jones, the librarian at King's, was likewise, helpful and supportive. Eleanor Vallis at Nuffield College, Oxford, was indispensable in helping me through Hubert Henderson's papers. Shealy Sieck and Lisa Adkins at Grinnell College processed an endless stream of inter-library loan requests with friendly efficiency. Christopher McKee, the Grinnell College Librarian, provided me with domicile for the writing of the manuscript.

Permission to quote from the unpublished writings is as follows: for unpublished writings of J. M. Keynes copyright The Provost and Scholars of King's College, Cambridge 1996. Permission to quote from the unpublished writings of Frank Ramsey is provided by Jane Burch. Permission to quote from the unpublished writings of Hubert Henderson is provided by Sir Nicholas Henderson. Permission to quote from the unpublished letters of Lytton Strachey is provided by the Society of Authors as agents for the Strachey Trust. Crown Copyright material in the Public Record Office is reproduced by permission of the Controller of Her Majesty's Stationery Office. Permission to reprint "The Good Life," from his collection *Life Supports,* is provided by William Bronk. Cover drawing by David Levine. Reprinted with permission from *The New York Review of Books.* Copyright © 1968, Nyrev, Inc.

Financial assistance during the period I worked on the manuscript was provided by the National Endowment for the Humanities (Grants FE 27273-92 and FT 37854-93), the Grinnell College Grant Board, and the Rosenfield Program in Human Rights, International Affairs, and Public Policy. The book could not have been completed without the help of Jack and Lucille Harris; a Harris Fellowship provided a year away from my teaching to do archival work and to write most of the first draft of the manuscript.

Tom Baldwin and Margaret Paul read chapters 2 and 3 in earlier drafts and provided me with extensive comments. Peter Clarke, Donald Gillies, Abe Hirsch, Kevin Hoover, and Donald Moggridge read the penultimate draft and gave me invaluable suggestions for improvement. Terri Phipps, Carolyn Ossman, and Vicki Bunnell saw the manuscript through endless revisions and never complained. Colin Day provided more support than could be expected from any editor.

My greatest debt is to my family who supported me throughout. This book is dedicated to my wife.

Contents

Part 1
Introduction

Prologue

Putting Keynes in Context

This book tells the story of Maynard Keynes's concern with probability and uncertainty. Economists have been interested in Keynes's concern with these ideas for almost 35 years, since G. L. S. Shackle first argued in 1961 for the possibility of a relationship between Keynes's early work in *A Treatise on Probability* (1921a) and his later work in *The General Theory of Employment, Interest, and Money* (1936).[1] But for all their interest in these ideas, it seems fair to say that they still have not tried to tell the *story* behind Keynes's concern with them. Although the flow of books and articles on the topic has become increasingly sophisticated in the explication of Keynes's early philosophical work, they are virtually all in the traditional genre of doctrine histories; they attempt to nail down the exact nature of Keynes's analytical arguments, but they do not address the question of *where* Keynes's interest in the ideas came from.[2]

This narrow interest in Keynes's ideas is not surprising, since almost all work by economists in the history of economic thought is of exactly this nature. We tend to write *thin* histories of the analytical constructs of our ancestors and shy away from the kind of *thick* histories written by other historians.[3] It is impossible to say with certainty why this is the case, but the most likely reason is the desire of historians of economic

---

1. See Shackle 1961 and Patinkin 1990, 215–16.
2. Both Carabelli 1988 and O'Donnell 1989 offer some historical background, but their basic style of argument is that of analytical philosophy. That is to say, once they have identified the single model (or framework) that they argue defines Keynes's thinking on probability, they then proceed to write largely about the model (or framework) and how it can be found embedded in his economics. Some economists who write about Keynes make no pretense of being interested in his ideas for historical purposes. See, for instance, Runde 1994.
3. The terminology of thick and thin histories of economics comes from McCloskey 1988.

3

thought not to be further marginalized by other economists.[4] Since the Second World War, academic economists have nearly abandoned a historical approach to economic questions and have focused intensively on technical theoretical questions and quantitative models. In order to avoid being completely bypassed by this mainstream focus on technique, historians of economics have largely abandoned the tradition of placing economic ideas in a broader cultural context or examining the role of those ideas in the larger society, choosing instead to focus on the pedigrees of specific analytical ideas. In fact, the late George Stigler, a Nobel Prize–winning theorist who also doubled as a historian of economic thought, made this stricture explicit; he argued that histories of economics were only valuable to the extent that they focused on the internal theoretical structures of academic economists and ignored the external influences on their thought.[5]

In trying to tell the story of Keynes's interest I am necessarily forced to abandon this thin approach. My purpose, however, is not to focus solely on the external influences on Keynes's theoretical work. Far from it. If anything, the ideas are still at center stage. But without considering the external influences, it simply is not possible to get Keynes's ideas in clear focus.[6] Understanding the flawed nature of his early Platonism, for instance, is essential to understanding why he later abandoned his core ideas in *A Treatise on Probability*. But it is difficult to understand why Keynes would have adopted such an obviously flawed idea without understanding the complex nature of his relationship to the philosopher G. E. Moore. Likewise, it is impossible to understand Keynes's use of uncertainty in *The General Theory* without understanding his long and protracted battle in the early 1930s over the importance of business confidence to the Slump.

---

4. One can imagine, of course, that *both* internalist and externalist histories of economics would have value. But while I believe that a history that tells a full story of the history of an idea will almost always be more interesting and useful, I am not arguing that purely internalist histories of the discipline have no value. What I am addressing here is the question of why such histories are virtually the only kind written by economists. For examples of exceptions that prove the rule, see S. K. Howson and D. Winch 1977; W. J. Barber 1990; or Moggridge 1992.

5. In fact, Stigler's argument is more complex than a simple preference for the internal over the external. He argues further that the only legitimate framework for an internal history is *contemporary* theoretical ideas, rather than those of the original author. See Stigler 1976b. Interestingly, Paul Samuelson, the other Nobel Laureate who doubles as a historian of economics also argues for the supremacy of Whig histories. See Samuelson 1987.

6. For a similar argument see Moggridge 1986, 1992.

The best way to tell this story would undoubtedly be to write it as a straight narrative history. This is what I have tried to do, but with one important improvisation. To highlight the mix of influences and ambitions in Keynes's work, I have relied on a device that is used more frequently by historians of science than it is by historians of economics. This device is the distinction mentioned above between internal and external influences. Although the story I am trying to tell could be told without any reference to these two terms, I have chosen to use them because I think they highlight the story behind Keynes's interest in probability and uncertainty.

But just as this vocabulary offers the benefit of emphasizing my point about the necessity of putting Keynes's ideas in context, there are also costs involved in using it. The first, and most important, cost is that the story may be less fluid than it would otherwise be. The worst thing about academic prose is that it is full of jargon. Another possible cost is the artificial precision that comes with using any theoretical framework. Sometimes the influences on Keynes were clearly external; sometimes they were clearly internal. But there are times when it is difficult to tell how to categorize the complex of changes and influences at work on him. Thus my point in using this vocabulary is not to insist that it neatly explains everything in my story. My point is to persuade you that seeing Keynes's ideas in a broader context helps in understanding them more clearly.

There is some irony that the vocabulary I have chosen to help me in this persuasion is drawn from the history of science, since I have drawn much more heavily from political historians, philosophers, and economic historians than I have from historians of science in building my story. But while I hope historians of science find this book of interest, it is more likely, given the accident of current academic habits, that my readers outside the discipline of economics will be political historians and philosophers.[7] These are the people who are now writing about Keynes in new and intriguing ways, and I have tried to tell a story that will be as compelling to them as it is to my fellow economists. The time has passed when one can write a good history of any part of Keynes's life that does not also draw on the work being done in these other disciplines.

But, in the end, the particular way in which I have told this story is undoubtedly colored by the fact that I am an economist. This book is written by an economist, for economists. Unlike the typical argument by

---

7. Margaret Schabas (1992) nicely explains the things that differentiate the current work of historians of science from that of historians of economic thought.

economists who write doctrine histories, however, my purpose is neither to lionize, nor to repudiate, Keynes's theories. I am trying to argue neither that we should resurrect one of his theoretical models, nor that his work was destructive (to the profession or the Western economies). Keynes had good and bad ideas, and we can be frank about this.

My point, for economists, is a broader one. The story of his interest in probability and uncertainty points to the richness of the process of scientific discovery. Keynes brought a variety of interests to his work that made it richer and better. Economists have finally begun to admit to themselves that their work is thinner and less useful than it might be exactly because it neglects the richness of influences that Keynes brought to his work.[8] By neglecting history, policy, politics, and philosophy, economists have run the risk of irrelevance.[9] Thus, while I hope that my explorations of political history and philosophy will be of interest to historians and philosophers, I especially hope that economists will see in this story some of the value that lies in doing work that is worthy of being retold for a later generation.

---

8. One can now safely say that mainstream, postwar economics has become too technical without being taken to argue that mathematics or technique are bad for economics, per se. The room for this kind of critical thinking has been created by none other than some of our best theorists. Kenneth Arrow (1985), William Baumol (1990, 1991), and Robert Solow (1985) have all argued that economic theory is now poorer for having abandoned its traditional link to economic history. See also J. A. Miron 1991.

9. One concrete bit of evidence of this irrelevance is in the final report of the Committee on Graduate Education in Economics of the American Economic Association, where it is reported that there is a decreasing demand for economists in some areas. See Anne Krueger et. al. 1991 and W. Lee Hansen 1991. See also the widely cited article by Robert Kuttner (1985).

CHAPTER 1

Das Maynard Keynes Problem

Near the end of the nineteenth century, German economists were struck by an apparent paradox in the history of economic ideas: reading Adam Smith's two great works, *The Theory of Moral Sentiments* and *The Wealth of Nations*, they wondered how the person who made sympathy the mainspring of human action in the first book could also be the person who made calculating self-interest the primary motive force of the second book. How could one reconcile the advocate of sympathy with the advocate of self-interest? Thus arose *das Adam Smith problem*.

In retrospect, the end of the twentieth century will have produced a paradox of equal concern. A century from now, when the names and nationalities of today's scholars are forgotten, economists, philosophers, and historians will wonder over how the person who wrote *A Treatise on Probability* could also have been the author of *The General Theory of Employment, Interest and Money*. They will read the first book's account of the objective nature of probabilities and the way that rational people employ them, and they will wonder at how this person could have turned around 15 years later and written a book in which irrational people who base their decisions on social conventions cause mass unemployment in the capitalist system. Books about *das Maynard Keynes problem* will be just as common in 2095 as books about das Adam Smith problem are today.[1]

The books on Maynard Keynes will necessarily be more complex and involved, however. For while Smith's work was no less influential or complex than Keynes's, we know more about Keynes than we do about Smith. Beyond his teaching, Keynes was actively involved in shaping economic policy and the emerging institutions meant to measure and control economic activity. Smith, on the other hand, became directly involved with the economy only late in his life, and then only as a customs inspector who had no influence on policy.[2] Even more

---

1. Two of the best recent books to discuss das Adam Smith problem are by Albert O. Hirschman (1977) and Richard F. Teichgraeber (1986).
2. See Robert D. Tollison 1984.

important than the lives they led is what the two men left us in the form of documents, letters, and other archival material. Smith left almost nothing; he even had what might have been his magnum opus, 16 folio volumes of manuscripts upon which he had worked for years, destroyed shortly before his death.[3] Keynes, conversely, saved virtually everything and left it all for us.

But while it might seem that this larger amount of material would make it easier to understand the evolution of Keynes's thought, this has not turned out to be the case. Despite the tens of thousands of documents that Keynes left, the burgeoning literature on his philosophical thought is noteworthy largely for its lack of agreement about the nature or import of any facet of his work. Thus, while Anna Carabelli, Athol Fitzgibbons, and Roderick O'Donnell each argue that Keynes's philosophical ideas remained unchanged between *Probability* and the *General Theory,* they vehemently disagree over what the nature of that unchanged philosophy is.[4] Likewise, while Anna Carabelli and Ted Winslow find organicism to be a major theme of Keynes's work, they disagree on the meaning of organicism and its place in his economics.[5]

This disagreement among scholars, despite the tremendous amount of information still extant, is probably not surprising. Indeed, it is the "natural" room for disagreement and the seeming inevitability of different interpretations that makes so plausible the prediction that there will be a das Maynard Keynes problem in 100 years. What *is* surprising is that virtually the entire body of this emerging literature repudiates the unambiguous statements that Keynes made following the publication of *Probability* about how and why his philosophical ideas subsequently changed.[6] Virtually none of the recent work on Keynes accepts his own statement that he abandoned his earlier conception of probability in the face of Frank Ramsey's attack in *The Foundations of Mathematics.* Virtually none of the recent work accepts his own statement in "My Early Beliefs" that he saw his earlier attachment to Platonism as a mistake.[7] Nor does any of the recent work accept his related statements in "My

---

3. See Teichgraeber 1986, 138.
4. See Carabelli 1988; Fitzgibbons 1988; and O'Donnell 1989. My essay (Bateman 1991b) contains a review of all three of these works.
5. See Carabelli 1988 and Winslow 1986. See John Davis 1989 for an argument that organicism as understood by Carabelli and Winslow was not central to Keynes's thought.
6. The exceptions to this tide include John Davis (1989, 1991a, 1991b), Allin Cottrell (1993), and Donald Gillies (1988).
7. "My Early Beliefs," in *Two Memoirs* (1949).

Early Beliefs" that the fundamental error in his early work was the attribution of rationality to people.

This repudiation of Keynes's statements about the changes in his thinking is one of the reasons that the space for this book exists. It is not just that there appears to be a das Maynard Keynes problem to the careful reader of *Probability* and the *General Theory;* Keynes himself offered ample evidence of, and explanation for, the changes in his ideas between the publication of his *magna opera;* one purpose of this book is to use those statements to reconstruct the story of how Keynes's philosophical ideas changed.

But the neglect of Keynes's statements about how his philosophical thinking changed is not the only reason that space exists for this book. In the large literature on Keynes's concern with uncertainty, virtually no attention has been paid to the influence of his extensive work in policy making. The explicit, or implicit, assumption has been that Keynes's early work in *Probability* provided him with an analytical framework or set of concerns that lay dormant until *The General Theory;* the question of what experiences in his life might have spurred his return to uncertainty 15 years after the publication of *Probability* has simply not been asked.[8] Thus, another purpose of this book is to trace the impact of Keynes's concern with policy making on his thinking about the importance of confidence and uncertainty to economic decisions.

When these two unexplored areas are considered together the result is an unexpected story of the importance of rules and conventions to Keynes's thought. This is one of the themes around which "My Early Beliefs" is built, and it turns out to be crucial to an understanding of the evolution of Keynes's ideas. Two stories that might, a priori, seem unrelated, turn out to be linked by a common thread. Keynes originally became interested in the study of probability as a means of *repudiating* the need to obey general rules of conduct. After he had changed his mind about the nature of probability and applied his new conception of probability to economic behavior, he found that it led him to emphasize the necessity of rules and social conventions to the successful maintenance of modern capitalism. In both cases, the nature of probability and the necessity of rules are inextricably intertwined.

---

8. The first person to note this lacuna in the literature on Keynes and probability was D. E. Moggridge (1986). Skidelsky (1992) can be said to offer an effort to fill the lacuna, but his account neglects Keynes's early connection to Cambridge trade cycle theory and his long, trenchant opposition to the use of business confidence in explanations of the Slump.

Even with the aid of this focus on the role of rules in Keynes's thought, however, it is not possible to tell a simple linear story. At each turn of the story Keynes rejects and embraces new and old ideas. For anyone with a passing familiarity with the evolution of Keynes's economic thought from *A Tract on Monetary Reform* to *A Treatise on Money* to the *General Theory,* this will come as no surprise. Keynes constantly reworked and reformulated economic theory to meet the theoretical and practical problems that his previous efforts had encountered. If he was often arrogant or imperious in his relationships with individuals who tried to persuade him of the errors in his work, he was just as often generous and cooperative with his critics, and this betrays his deeper concern for "getting it right." He was willing to challenge the merits of a particular argument—his own, as well as others'.

The fact that Keynes's economic ideas were constantly changing and shifting will perhaps lead the reader to wonder if the changes in his philosophical ideas were a *cause* for the changes in his economic ideas. Ultimately, this does not seem to be the case. I argue that his use of probability in the *General Theory* was an externally determined application of changes that had already taken place in his philosophical thinking; that is, his work in policy making convinced him of the importance of uncertainty and led him to see the efficacy of using his changed ideas about probability.[9]

Because I do not believe that the changes in Keynes's economic thinking were determined by the changes in his philosophical thinking, I have not included a fresh (or stale) argument about the exact evolution of his economic ideas from the *Treatise* to the *General Theory.* This is the most worked over ground in Keynesian scholarship and that least necessary of reworking; the excellent, but disparate, accounts of Peter Clarke, Robert Dimand, Don Moggridge, and Don Patinkin are all fundamentally compatible with the story I am telling. What matters for the telling of my story is that by late 1933 the primary analytical elements of the *General Theory* were in place in Keynes's mind; at that point, his growing concern with the importance of business confidence could be embodied in his newly derived analytical framework in the

---

9. My argument that Keynes's changing philosophical ideas were not the cause of his changing economic ideas is in sharp contradistinction to O'Donnell's (1989) argument that Keynes had an overarching philosophical schema that drove his economics. One serious flaw with O'Donnell's argument is that it cannot account for Keynes's changing attitude toward the importance of businessmen's expectations to macroeconomic performance.

guise of the intersubjective probabilities that he had come to embrace following Ramsey's critique of his earlier ideas.

Thus, rather than retell, in detail, the story of the transition from the *Tract* to the *Treatise* to the *General Theory*, I have attempted, in chapters 4 and 5, to provide an account of Keynes's early concern with uncertainty, from roughly 1910 to 1923, and the subsequent changes in his economic thinking that brought him to the point in 1933 that he could then incorporate his changed philosophical ideas into his analytical organon. Once he was finally convinced of the importance of business confidence, the groundwork was laid for introducing his changed philosophical ideas to his economics.

I have titled this book *Keynes's Uncertain Revolution* because of the nice ambiguity of the phrase. Keynes was instrumental in a revolution that has brought uncertainty to the center of macroeconomic theory, as well as being the father of a revolution in economic policy that has very uncertain implications. The first sense of revolution concerns the question of *theoretical* revolution. Keynes occupies a preeminent position in twentieth-century macroeconomics for being the first theorist to successfully model how the short-run level of output is determined; and he always claimed that the introduction of uncertainty was an integral part of this theoretical revolution. In historical retrospect, however, considerable uncertainty accompanies his claim regarding the introduction of uncertainty. The Cambridge tradition of monetary analysis had always involved a concern with uncertainty, and Cambridge trade cycle theory was *grounded* in a concern with uncertainty. Keynes had been an adherent of these earlier theories and thus knew that his statements about his interest in uncertainty were merely provocative pieces of hyperbole. He may have extended and formalized the concerns of his teacher, Alfred Marshall, but he did not invent the revolution he claimed for himself. Ironically, Keynes's loose interpretation of the historical record has been justly repaid, for while macroeconomics in the late twentieth century has been largely focused on uncertainty and expectations, the theorists who wrought this later revolution worked in near total ignorance of Keynes's concern with uncertainty. Indeed, the foot soldiers in the Rational Expectations revolution advanced uncertainty as a theoretical innovation that could topple Keynesian economics!

The second sense of revolution concerns a revolution in economic policy: the policies of demand management and state intervention in the economy that we associate with Keynes's name. One sense in which we are uncertain about this revolution is the extent to which it is correctly attributable to Keynes. Much recent scholarship points to the fact that most Western democracies adapted demand-management policies with little or no direct influence from Keynes's writing; it seems much more the case that his name was attached to the changes after the fact.[10] Another sense in which we are uncertain about this revolution in economic policy involves its practical value in light of the great stagflation of the 1970s. The concern that arose then with inflation and fiscal deficits (following the oil price shocks) is widely seen as the point at which Keynesian demand-management policies lost their legitimacy.

The main point of my argument about this second sense of the Keynesian revolution lies elsewhere, however. I am concerned with the extent to which it can be argued, *for Keynes's part,* that the trade cycle could be controlled by activist fiscal policy, or the active use of the government budget. Many people have begun to call this interpretation of the Keynesian revolution into question, and this book aims to provide a further undergirding to those who argue against the traditional idea that *The General Theory* is a book written primarily to defend the use of activist fiscal policy.[11]

But finally, the uncertainty in Keynes's revolution lies in our inability to understand exactly what he intended. While I am certain that our understanding of his intentions is furthered by taking the changes in his philosophical thinking seriously and by considering the influence of his experience in policy making, I am not certain that the full story is the one I have told here, for there is a fundamental indeterminacy in the retelling of that story. This stems, in part, from the phenomenal diversity of Keynes's interests and activities and the resulting need to use the expertise of many disciplines to gain a full understanding of his work.

At an even deeper level, however, it stems from the fact that Keynes found himself by the late 1930s with a set of sentiments and ideas accumulated over a lifetime but with no good way to express these. Nowhere is this more clear than in his ideas about rationality.

---

10. The essays in Peter Hall's volume (1989) point most directly to the lack of a direct link between Keynes's writings and the rise of macroeconomic management. Stigler (1976a) was certainly one of the first to question this link. The two countries where a strong case for Keynes's direct influence can be made are the United Kingdom and Canada.

11. Among those who question whether *The General Theory* was a book written to advocate activist fiscal policy are David Colander (1984) and Allan Meltzer (1988). Peter Clarke's (1988) last chapter argues persuasively that Keynes's general level of activism after *The General Theory* was considerably less than that of the Keynesians in postwar academe.

Early in his life, under the sway of G. E. Moore's Platonist influence, he had taken rationality to have a very narrow meaning: people always act so as to achieve what is objectively and recognizably *good.*

We were among the last of the Utopians, or meliorists as they are sometimes called, who believe in a continuing moral progress by virtue of which the human race already consists of reliable, rational, decent people, influenced by truth and objective standards, who can be safely released from the outward restraints of convention and traditional standards and inflexible rules of conduct, and left, from now onwards, to their own sensible devices, pure motives and reliable intuitions of the good. The view that human nature is reasonable had in 1903 quite a long history behind it. It underlay the ethics of self-interest—rational self-interest as it was called—just as much as the universal ethics of Kant or Bentham which aimed at the general good; and it was because self-interest was *rational* that the egoistic and altruistic systems were supposed to work out in practice to the same conclusions.[12]

Later in his life, however, despite having abandoned Platonism and the idea that good is an objective quality of things, Keynes still found himself prone to lapsing into speaking as if rationality could be defined in the earlier sense in which he had imagined it.

As cause and consequence of our general state of mind we completely misunderstood human nature, including our own. The rationality which we attributed to it led to a superficiality, not only of judgment, but also of feeling. It was not only that intellectually we were pre-Freudian, but we had lost something which our predecessors had without replacing it. I still suffer incurably from attributing an unreal rationality to other people's feelings and behaviour (and doubtless to my own, too). There is one small but extraordinarily silly manifestation of this absurd idea of what is "normal," namely the impulse to *protest*—to write a letter to *The Times,* call a meeting in the Guildhall, subscribe to some fund when my presuppositions as to what is "normal" are not fulfilled. I behave as if there really existed some authority or standard to which I can

---

12. Keynes 1949, 98–99.

successfully appeal if I shout loud enough—perhaps it is some hereditary vestige of a belief in the efficacy of prayer.[13]

Thus, by Keynes's own lights, we find him later in his life "protesting and praying" for a point of view to which he no longer actually subscribed.[14] Although the "objective" basis for "rational" action had been removed, Keynes still wanted people to act so as to bring about a good world; when they didn't he called them "irrational." Shorn of the certainty of his early beliefs, he was left to express himself imperfectly. This indeterminacy arising from the loss of his early beliefs leads to the final uncertainty about the Keynesian revolution. Because Keynes lost the certainty of his early vocabulary, scholars will always be faced with the dilemma of trying to discern his actual beliefs from the imperfect approximations he found for his own thoughts. My own argument rests on the belief that Keynes meant what he said when he abandoned his early, naive concept of rationality. It seems certain, however, that the ambiguity in his language means that das Maynard Keynes problem will remain a part of the history of economic thought for as long as we remain concerned with Keynes himself.

---

13. Ibid., 100.

14. O'Donnell (1989, 148) argues that "My Early Beliefs" is "possibly the most deceptive document in Keynes's *oeuvre*, flawed by error, vagueness, internal inconsistency, and hyperbole." This allegation is unpersuasive, however, for while the memoir is clearly written for a group of insiders (i.e., Bloomsburies) and so employs both humor and hyperbole, it very accurately portrays the broad outlines of Keynes's early attachment to Platonism.

Part 2
Keynes and Probability

Prologue to Part 2

The first step in understanding Keynes's work in probability is to try to understand the unique, and peculiar, approach that he took to the subject. His interest in the *philosophical* question of the status of uncertain knowledge took him in a direction in which he had few predecessors. At the time he first approached the topic, he refused to accept the prevailing idea that probability refers to the percentage of times that something occurs in repeated trials. Beyond this basic intuition, however, he had no clear idea of how to proceed.

Thus, the first part of the story of his interest in probability is trying to uncover the process by which he constructed a new, alternative conception of probability. This took Keynes approximately three years, though he was by no means working exclusively on this problem during the interim. In fact, it was only after a circuitous process of arguing through the ideas of the Cambridge philosopher G. E. Moore that Keynes came to adopt the philosophical position on which he built his new system.

Unfortunately, the argument he used to undergird his new theory of probability, Platonism, turned out to be fatally flawed. Other philosophers were quick to point out the untenable nature of Keynes's argument, and *A Treatise on Probability* has never had an active following.

Not even Keynes himself could keep the faith. In the face of criticism from his friend and fellow Cambridge philosopher, Frank Ramsey, Keynes capitulated in 1931 and admitted that the *objective* probability relations that he posited in his book simply did not exist. Although he still believed that people rarely (if ever) acted on the basis of the frequency with which things happened, he now had to admit that the basis for their actions was *subjective,* rather than objective.

This capitulation to Ramsey offers the clear first step in the solution to das Maynard Keynes problem, for Keynes's conception of rational behavior in *A Treatise on Probability* was dependent on the existence of objective probabilities. If people could not act in accordance with these objective probabilities, there was no basis for rational action. But while this can help to explain the shift in Keynes's position between *Probability* and *The General Theory*, it still leaves open the question of how Keynes's subjective probabilities became embedded in the latter book. This second step in the story must wait for Part 3.

CHAPTER 2

Converting to Moorism, Twice

The story of Maynard Keynes's life in the first decade of this century is not an easy one for the modern reader to conjure. We feel certain that something that happened in the twentieth century must be accessible to us; but when we consider that it was almost a century ago, we begin to wonder. Recent scholarship has begun to suggest the difficulties involved. Paul Fussell's highly celebrated *The Great War and Modern Memory,* for instance, reminds us that the cultural presuppositions of Europe before the First World War are almost lost to us today. Keynes's own *Economic Consequences of the Peace* (1920), of course, depends heavily on the idea that the West had been irrevocably changed by the loss of those pre-war presuppositions, and now, 75 years later, we wonder at our ability to fully understand what was lost.

It did not take a hundred years, however, for contemporary readers to forget what Keynes's turn-of-the-century world was like. In the fall of 1938, when Keynes sat down to write his essay, "My Early Beliefs," for the Memoir Club, he found it possible to reflect on the fact that the younger members (all second-generation Bloomsburies) probably knew nothing of the intellectual currents that had defined his own generation.

> I went up to Cambridge at Michaelmas 1902, and Moore's *Principia Ethica* came out at the end of my first year. I have never heard of the present generation having read it.[1]

And, indeed, he spends nearly as much time in the memoir explicating Moore's philosophy as he does explaining its influence, since he doubts that his audience knows what Moore is about. "Even if the new members of the club know what the religion was (do they?), it will not do any of us any harm to try and recall the crude outlines."

---

1. Keynes 1949, 81.

If we can extend Keynes's presumption and assume that *Principia Ethica* is still not widely read, then it seems that a reader today likewise needs to consider that Moore and his influence is the most likely place to begin an inquiry into Keynes's early beliefs. If we extend Keynes's religion metaphor, however, this is not a simple conversion story. Although Keynes himself does not discuss it in his essay, he became a Moorite *twice,* once in 1903 and again in 1906. If we consider both of these conversions, and his interim rejection of Moorism, we can at least begin to gain some perspective on Keynes's life in the first decade of this century. Such a treatment will not ultimately resolve questions of the extent to which he was a late-Victorian as opposed to a true Edwardian, much less provide an adequate treatment of those milieus. But because so much of Moore's influence on Keynes was of a personal nature (even when it was manifest analytically), a full understanding of Keynes's two conversions provides an important framework for understanding his early life and his original interest in probability.

Rejecting Moore

Keynes's first conversion to Moorism is a well-rehearsed story.[2] He came to Cambridge in the fall of 1902 and was almost immediately vetted for the secret society known as the Apostles. Admitted in February 1903, he became a member with such notable figures as Lytton Strachey, Leonard Woolf, and John Sheppard, all of whom were under the spell of Moore and his work. "The influence was not only overwhelming; but it was the extreme opposite of what Strachey used to call *funeste;* it was exciting, exhilarating, the beginning of a renaissance, the opening of a new heaven on a new earth, we were the forerunners of a new dispensation, we were not afraid of anything." All these young men were attracted by Moore's moral character, especially his earnestness, and by the special emphasis he put on the ethical nature of beauty and friendship. But while Moore's aesthetic interests formed a real and lasting influence on the Apostles and Bloomsbury, it is much more his interest in friendship that attracts modern attention. As Bloomsbury has become a small cottage industry for scholars and journalists, interest in the personal lives, especially the sexual relations, of the Bloomsburies has become paramount.

In retrospect, however, it is unfair to limit Moore's influence solely

---

2. Keynes (1949) tells this story best himself. See also Harrod 1951 and Skidelsky 1985.

to the sphere of friendship (or of art); indeed, I will go on to argue that in Keynes's case there is a deep and lasting *analytical* influence.[3] Nonetheless, this well-rehearsed story of Keynes's attraction to Moore and his ideas serves as a reasonable description of Keynes's first conversion to Moorism. It was the strong commitments to friendship and aesthetic enjoyment, taken to the extreme of unworldliness, that first attracted Keynes and made him an ardent disciple.

The story that is not so well rehearsed, which is, in fact, not explained in the literature, is how Keynes came to reject a large part of "Moorism" in the next three years.[4]

The initial reason for this rejection is reasonably straightforward and well documented in Keynes's unpublished letters and manuscripts from the period: he became personally disenchanted with Moore and found Moore's "Method" to be detrimental to recruiting new Apostles. But this kind of story does not fit easily into the way that historians of economic thought are accustomed to describing the evolution of a person's ideas. When historians of economic thought discuss the growth and changes in someone's ideas, they typically describe a sequence of theoretical models and focus on the differences between these models; what happens to the economist apart from what goes onto the page is just not a part of the story.[5]

An excellent example of this kind of work would be the typical study of how Keynes's ideas changed between the *Treatise on Money* and the *General Theory*. It is commonplace, for instance, to explain that because the *Treatise* tries to describe macroeconomic phenomena, while

---

3. Paul Levy (1979) asserts that Moore's influence on Keynes was personal rather than analytical. The subsequent explosion of research on Keynes's early philosophical writing has shown Levy's remark to be unfounded. See, for instance, Bateman 1988.

4. O'Donnell (1989, 13–15) comes closest to seeing the story I recount here, though he offers no elaboration or explanation of Keynes's changing position. He says, "Keynes never desisted from disagreeing with *Principia Ethica* whenever he found himself unable to accept its doctrines, the latter half of 1905 being a period of particularly close critical assessment. But by January 1906, most of his doubts had receded and his earlier ecstatic admiration of Moore revived. . . ." O'Donnell makes no mention, however, of Keynes's disenchantment with "Moore's Method"; and he labels the distinction that Keynes makes between "goodness" and "fitness" in several of his early essays as a mere "refinement" of Moore's analysis, rather than pointing to the deeper philosophical split that is connoted by the distinction. John Davis (1991, 62–70) offers an excellent explanation of Keynes's early criticism of Moore that helps to show that it was not a "refinement."

5. Although I disagree with George Stigler's (1976b) argument that an economist's biography has no legitimate bearing on our understanding of his work, it is difficult to argue with his many examples of how biography has been used poorly in trying to explicate someone's work.

assuming that output does not change, it provides an inadequate model of an economy that suffers the severe swings of the business cycle and that this led to the need for a new model that could explain those swings in output and employment. Historians of science describe explanations of this type as *internalist* history. The term is meant to denote the fact that the changes being described are internal to the discipline or derive from failings with the theories as theories.

The story of Keynes's rejection of Moorism, however, has both internal and external elements. In the first place, Keynes never rejected the Moorean desiderata of beauty and friendship. In this sense Keynes's story in "My Early Beliefs" is not misleading or false, as Roderick O'Donnell has asserted; Keynes adhered to these "habits of feeling" all his life.[6] What Keynes revolted against first was the use of "Moore's method" in everyday conversation and this, in turn, led to his rejection of one of the foundations of Moore's philosophy. But initially this rejection did not stem from any failing of Moore's work as a philosophical theory; that is, it was not tested according to some philosophical criteria and found wanting. Keynes's initial reason for rejecting Moore was external to the discipline of philosophy and the standards by which philosophers normally accept or reject theories. Historians of science would label this part of the story as *externalist.*

The external circumstance that led to this rejection was the moribund state of the Apostles in the three years following Keynes's election. Relatively overlooked in the descriptions of the euphoria that fill every narrative of the Apostles in this period is the fact that only one new member was elected between February 1903 and February 1906.[7] The forerunners of this new dispensation may have been quite exhilarated, but they were not attracting the kind of new blood that was crucial to the continued life of the society.

The suspected culprit in this dearth of new Apostles was Moore's method. Keynes and Lytton Strachey, in particular, and Sheppard to a lesser extent, all employed what they took to be Moore's distinctive method of philosophical analysis as a tool for identifying and recruiting new members. In his memoir, Keynes describes how this method was used in discussions between members of the society.

> It was all under the influence of Moore's method, according to which you could hope to make essentially vague notions clear by

---

6. See O'Donnell 1989, 148.
7. Levy (1979, 300–310) contains a list of Apostles up to the First World War.

using precise language about them and asking exact questions. It was a method of discovery by the instrument of impeccable grammar and an unambiguous dictionary. "What *exactly* do you mean?" was the phrase most frequently on our lips. If it appeared under cross-examination that you did not mean *exactly* anything, you lay under a strong suspicion of meaning nothing whatever. It was a stringent education in dialectic; but in practice it was a kind of combat in which strength of character was really much more valuable than subtlety of mind. In the preface to his great work, bespattered with the numerous italics through which the reader who knew him could actually hear, as with Queen Victoria, the vehemence of his utterance, Moore begins by saying that error is chiefly "the attempt to answer questions, without first discovering precisely *what* question it is which you desire to answer. . . . Once we recognize the exact meaning of the two questions, I think it also becomes plain exactly what kind of reasons are relevant as arguments for or against any particular answer to them." So we spent our time trying to discover *precisely what* questions we were asking, confident in the faith that, if only we could ask precise questions, everyone would know the answer.[8]

It is not difficult to imagine how this "combat" might easily have thrown up a barrier to the recruitment of new members. New members were always vetted in a series of meetings—breakfasts, lunches, teas— in which the real purpose of the meeting was unknown to them. One can almost see some poor twenty-year-old, sitting in rooms in King's or Trinity, not really sure why he has been invited to be there, being put through a difficult interview in which the interviewers believe they are pursuing truth via tough questioning, but in fact are engaged in a battle of personalities. When one then adds into the picture that a large part of the interview was meant to ascertain the guest's sexual preference, the situation appears nearly hopeless. The chance seems very dim that someone would rise to the occasion, see the "stringent dialectic" itself as an object of desire, and engage Maynard and Lytton in the type of conversation that they so coveted.

The problems are clear in the Strachey-Keynes correspondence of this period.[9] Following Moore's departure from Cambridge for Edin-

---

8. Keynes 1949, 88–89.

9. All of the quotations cited here in the correspondence between Keynes and Lytton Strachey are from original letters in file PP/45 in the Keynes Papers.

burgh in the fall of 1904, after his Fellowship at Trinity College came to an end, there developed a certain distance between Moore and the active Apostles. Moore had always manifest a propensity to sink into silence at Apostles' meetings when he was unsure of *exactly* what to say, and his physical removal may have seemed like one long brooding silence to those left behind in Cambridge.

J. M. K. to Lytton Strachey, 1 January 1905

Moore will never be able to live up to his myth, if things go much further and he stays in Edinburgh much longer.

Lytton Strachey to J. M. K., 11 January 1905

Moore has been here since Saturday and goes to Edinburgh today. He has gone. The wretched creature said he had no intention of coming to Cambridge next term, but that he would have to in the May term, as he's examining in the Tripos. This is rather disappointing, isn't it?

But what may have begun as pique and jealousy was a full-fledged revolt by the end of the year.

J. M. K. to Lytton Strachey, 6 November 1905

The great days are gone—for there were comparatively great days once. I foresee no remedy without a new method. There must be a new method: something that will bring ease. . . .

Lytton Strachey to J. M. K., 8 November 1905

The shocking thing is that even our intellect's in rather a hole. That damned Moorism has introduced a sort of orthodoxy into things which makes discussion on the big things impossible; and the little things which can still be discussed are so abominably difficult.

Though, properly understood, it was the *means,* not the *end,* of Moorism that was rotten. The affected, impeccable grammar that they took for their method of discussion was an unworkable social device.

J. M. K. to Lytton Strachey, 9 November 1905

We *must* give up Moorism as a creed—though, of course, we shall believe it all the same.

At this point in the correspondence, personal attacks on Moore reenter, but not as pique or jealousy. Keynes recounts a story he attributes to R. C. Trevelyan about Moore's poverty as an undergraduate and "the shocking confession that up to the very last moment the Society could scarcely decide whether to elect him because they couldn't be sure whether he was good enough." Strachey's reply is equally damning, "Oh yes, I can quite believe that the Society before Moore only elected him by accident." On the whole, however, the correspondence through the remainder of the year moves off the personal level and returns to a lament about the failure of Moore's method, per se.

J. M. K. to Lytton Strachey, 7 December 1905

I want to make a move against our methods—for I don't think that we're at all corrupt within. As it is we aren't—en bloc—fit company for the youth.

. . . To begin with one must learn to talk football or politics or metaphysics in general conversation and give up trying to make it an imitation of what one says nose to nose. For the same things seem to be decent nose to nose and a little immodest palem populo.[10]

Lytton Strachey to J. M. K., 9 December 1905

I agree with every word you say about the difficulties and depressions incident to our method.

For Keynes, at least, this revolt against Moore's method was the probable spur to a deeper revolution against one of the most important foundations of Moore's philosophy, the concept of indefinability. But while his rejection of Moore's method was clearly *external*, his rejection of indefinability has an uncertain pedigree; his working out of his critique in the papers written during the summer of 1905 is purely analytical. What we cannot know with certainty is whether Keynes was pushed to this (apparently internal) critique by his (external) frustration with Moore's method, al-

---

10. "Palem populo" can be translated as "in front of the people."

though his critical attitude to Moore would seem to have been an obvious spur to his analytical work.

The obvious place to look for evidence of this subsequent theoretical revolt might seem to be in Keynes's report in "My Early Beliefs" that he and the other younger Apostles at this time rejected the part of *Principia Ethica* that advocated the adherence to conventional rules of morality, a conclusion that Moore had reached in chapter 5. Evidence of this rejection does surface in a set of three Apostles papers read by Keynes in 1904 that all deal with the question of the need to follow rules.[11] The purpose of this earlier rejection of rules, however, was to throw over only a part of Moore's conclusions regarding correct behavior and to reinforce another conflicting part of those conclusions stipulating that individuals always have the right to consider what course of action is best in a particular case. Bertrand Russell had pointed to this inconsistency in Moore's argument in a 1904 review of *Principia,* and Keynes was pursuing the same line of attack in his 1904 papers. This rejection of Moore's argument for rules, then, is not a revolution against Moore, per se, but rather an effort to eliminate internal inconsistency in his argument and strengthen the conclusion that an individual's pursuit of friendship and beauty is paramount.

Keynes's *analytical* rejection of Moorism comes, rather, in the summer of 1905 during the long vacation. This period, before the advent of modern tourism, when King's College was an empty and silent refuge in the summers, marks the first real explosion of Keynes's interest in philosophy, or at least his first truly prodigious output of philosophical work. In June, he finished the mathematical tripos and began, as Roy Harrod put it, a "quest for a way of life," which included the study of both economics and philosophy and the consideration of what route to follow—a second, part 2 tripos (in economics or moral sciences) or the civil service examination. Less than a month after finishing his tripos he was deeply immersed in philosophy—rereading *Principia Ethica,* reading Brentano, scouring journals, and, most significantly, writing notes of his thoughts. The notes reveal a concern with both Moore's method and the analytical problem of indefinability.

J. M. K. to Lytton Strachey, 8 July 1905

I have been re-reading *Principa Ethica* and want to write a long criticism of it—but it is doubtful whether I shall. Also Brentano's book, which Moore refers to in his preface.

---

11. These are treated in the following.

This latter is most eminent. He has practically arrived at Moorism but without the Method—or at least he has a different method.

J. M. K. to Lytton Strachey, 20 July 1905

I purchased the *Revue de Metaphysique et de Morale* for May last to read an article I wanted, and behold I found a long review of *Principia Ethica*, which has, I suppose just penetrated to France. It was treated, it seems to me, with critical admiration; at least the cleverness was admitted: also a good deal had been understood and allowed: but the man had struck at the indefinability of good and at what Moore means by indefinability—he had some rather good criticisms.

The result of Keynes's submersion was two sets of notes—"Miscellanea Ethica," written during July–September, and "A Theory of Beauty," written during September–October—and a set of annotations in his copy of *Principia Ethica,* all dated in July.[12]

Examining the Indefinable

Ostensively, the purpose of Keynes's two papers written during the long vacation of 1905 was to correct what he took to be a taxonomic error in *Principia Ethica*. This hardly seems revolutionary. At the heart of Moore's book is the inquiry into what is good; indeed, he defines ethics itself as this inquiry. And Keynes, at first glance, only appears to want to make a semantical correction to Moore's results by more carefully distinguishing between what he terms *goodness* and *fitness*. Unlike Moore, who had argued that goodness could apply, for example, to a beautiful object, Keynes argued that goodness only applied to the states of mind that were the result of contemplating a beautiful object. In Keynes's conception, one's state of mind when one looks at a Picasso is *good* (that is, the feeling that it elicits in one may be termed good) whereas the painting itself is *fit*.[13] He makes his point clearly in his introduction to "Miscellanea Ethica."

---

12. Donald Gillies has pointed out to me the peculiarity that someone who had just taken a first in the mathematics tripos should pursue ethics and aesthetics as a first step in pursuing philosophy. In large part, this must represent the influence of Moore's ideas on Keynes at the time.

13. As Davis (1991b) explains, Keynes's papers are also concerned with the question of critiquing Moore's use of organic unities in *Principia Ethica*.

The predicate good is used by most ethical philosophers, including Mr. Moore though in a lesser degree, to express two notions which appear to me distinct. An object towards which a valuable mental relation is possible, is liable to receive the same epithet as the mental state it inspires. If the mental state which is "appropriate" to it is an unmixed good, then the object also is said to be good.

Anything which is fit to inspire a good feeling is itself regarded as good; on this principle beauty is a good, and many other wholes which partly or altogether involve non-mental elements. Further it is supposed that mental characteristics are fit to inspire good feelings in one who perceives them in exact proportion to their intrinsic goodness; —that we ought in fact to love the best we know.

Now I wish to distinguish the characteristics of the two constituents of the relation and, for the sake of convenience, to call the object of the feeling "fit" and the feeling itself "good."[14]

Keynes then goes on to further differentiate between the actual physical object and the mental image we have of it and to argue that it is, correctly speaking, only the mental image (i.e., the image formed in our mind) that is termed fit.

This distinction may help to explain Moore's eventual shift, in *Ethics* (1912), to the same position that only states of mind are properly termed good.[15] More importantly, it points to inconsistencies and problems in *Principia Ethica,* the most fundamental of which is Moore's "naive realism." This position, which has been described as everything from "unsatisfactory" to "absurd," represents the weakest point in Moore's examination of ethics and, in retrospect, seems the most obvious place to launch an attack on his book. Keynes's critiques of this position are tentative, but they illustrate that he understood the issues involved and worked them over extensively during the second half of 1905.

The naivety of Moore's argument in *Principia Ethica* refers to the belief he expresses there that good is a simple concept, indefinable in terms of anything else. This idea, which may seem relatively unobjectionable at first consideration, arose from Moore's critique of other ethical systems such as utilitarianism, which he took to identify good with some other thing in the world. The utilitarians, for instance, were taken to

---

14. File UA/21, Keynes Papers.
15. See Baldwin 1990, 130. It seems highly likely that the shift to speaking of "states of mind" in *Ethics* was the result of Bloomsbury's influence, via Keynes, on Moore. I am indebted to Tom Baldwin for first pointing this out to me.

identify good with pleasure, whereas Moore argued that pleasure might be either good or bad. Likewise, he argued against the advocates of evolutionary ethics, who identified all evolutionary change as good. Through use of his "impeccable grammar and unambiguous dictionary," Moore sought to whittle down good to being something different from any other predicate and so to dissociate it from any other idea or thing.

This, too, may seem relatively unobjectionable at first glance, but Moore's argument goes further. In the process of whittling down the *meaning* of the word *good*, Moore believed not just that he had isolated a unique meaning, or unique predicate, but that he had identified a *thing*.[16] He took good to be a real existing nonnatural entity or a Platonic form; this belief in Platonic forms is what is meant by "naive realism." Keynes could look back 30 years later and poke gentle fun at this "absurd" position.

> Moore had a nightmare once in which he could not distinguish propositions from tables. But even when he was awake, he could not distinguish love and beauty and truth from the furniture. They took on the same definition of outline, the same stable, solid, objective qualities and common-sense reality.[17]

Keynes was to come to embrace this Platonism himself, as he reports in "My Early Beliefs."

> I have called this faith a religion, and some sort of relation of neoplatonism it surely was. But we should have been very angry at the time with such a suggestion. We regarded all this as entirely rational and scientific in character. Like any other branch of science, it was nothing more than the application of logic and rational analysis to the material presented as sense-data.[18]

But this youthful embrace of Platonism came only after a studied period in which a critical approach to Moore and his work allowed Keynes to stand (momentarily) outside the Platonist fold.

Keynes's moment outside the Platonist fold came as a result of his critique of indefinability. Whereas Moore took the process of whittling predicates down to their simplest meaning to be identical to identifying

---

16. See Baldwin 1990, 72–74, 76 and Williams 1972, 52–54.
17. Keynes 1949, 94.
18. Ibid., 86.

a real existent Platonic entity, Keynes was skeptical that this process identified anything that existed outside the normally understood physical world. The most obvious example of this is in Keynes's treatment of the color yellow. Moore took "yellow" and "good" to be simple predicates that correspond to Platonic entities; Keynes denied in his work during this period that one could talk about yellow in isolation from its property of existing in the physical world. Keynes pursued his critique of indefinability to the point of insisting that any uniformity in our perception of qualities (predicates) was attributable to the similar capacities of human organs to sense the physical world, rather than to anything else.[19]

The first evidence we have of Keynes's concern with indefinability are his reading notes on the first chapter of *Principia Ethica*. These notes, on the inside back cover of Keynes's copy of the book (there are underlinings, but no notes, in the text itself), are dated from 1–2 July 1905.[20] They follow a consistent theme and illustrate the way in which one might circumvent Moore's Platonism. Whereas Moore sought to analyze and isolate the term *good* and then to declare that he had found a nonnatural Platonic entity, Keynes felt it might be possible to further analyze good and so find that it necessarily had other qualities that put it in a different realm. "If all good things are *necessarily* something else besides good, then good is analyzable; if they are only *actually* something else, then, it is true, that the unanalysability of good is unaffected." But the possibility that things are also *necessarily* something else loomed large in Keynes's mind.

> But suppose a prop*n*. of the form "all states wh. are good contain an element of happiness; but happiness is not the only good" could be found; if such a prop*n*. were "necessary," would not a step have been taken towards *analyzing* and *defining* good.

Keynes realized that it might be possible to find other characteristics of good things that would make it possible to prevent the reduction of good to one simple Platonic concept.

Later in the month, Keynes began the first of his two sets of notes, "Miscellanea Ethica," by pursuing this point.[21]

---

19. Davis (1991b, 66) distinguishes between Moore's position in *Principia Ethica* and Keynes's position in his critique of Moore as being the difference between *ethical objectivity* and *ethical subjectivity*.

20. Keynes's annotated copy of *Principia Ethica* is deposited in the Keynes Papers.

21. This essay is now deposited in file UA/21 in the Keynes Papers.

I shall discuss, in the first place, what Moore precisely means by the "indefinability" and "unanalysability" of good, and the proof he has put forward of the *impossibility* of ever finding a definition of the notion. With his refutation of various suggested definitions I am in complete agreement: I am with him when he denounces any ethical philosopher who should be imbued "with the conviction that good *can mean* nothing else than some *one* property of things." Good is not identical with any *one* thing except itself; but that does not prove that it may not be a complex notion. To prove that good is simple and indefinable, it is not sufficient to point out the naturalistic fallacy.

But what is meant by saying that a *quality* is simple or complex? Why is "sound" complex and "yellow" simple?

My difficulty is this:—the notion "yellow" seems to involve the notion "coloured" and some other notion which would seem to be unique and simple but which cannot be conceived in abstraction. In the same way "coloured" seems to involve the notion "spatially existent" and some other notion which cannot be conceived in abstraction. We seem to reach a point in analysis at which we arrive at a notion which can no longer be split up into notions which can be thought of apart. Such a notion we call simple. The important point to notice is that two simple notions may nevertheless have something in common.

In this sense I agree that "good" is simple; it involves a unique element which cannot be conceived in abstraction from the notion "good."

And if by "indefinable" it is meant that the notion cannot be *completely* explained by means of other notions capable of abstraction, then good is indefinable.

I do not know whether Moore means anything such as the above by "simple"; but this is the only sense in which I can see for myself that "good" is "simple."

But this interpretation allows me to admit the possibility of generalizations about "good" which are necessary and not merely actual. I can admit propositions of the form "x is good implies x is A" and not merely "everything that is good does, as a matter of fact, happen to be A."

I may without going to the trouble of inspecting *all* goods, be able to say something about "good" beyond simply "good is good."

I may, in fact, be able to establish a negative criterion of "good." I may be able to establish propositions derived from an analysis of the meaning of good of a form similar to

x is yellow implies x is coloured
x is coloured implies x is spatially existent
x is spatially existent implies x is existent
x is existent implies x has being
Each of these implications is established a priori from the essential
nature of the notions under consideration, and does not demand an
appeal to fact such as would be required by a proposition of the type:
x is yellow implies x is an orange
"Being" seems to me to be the only notion about which nothing
positive whatever can be said beyond "being is being." If I am inquir-
ing whether x is yellow and perceive that x is not spatially existent,
my question is answered at once. It will be an important step forward
if any such simplification can be introduced in the case of "good."

Keynes then proceeds to spend approximately 20 pages developing his
distinction between good and fit as a means of developing this thesis that
good may be complex. By arguing that goodness and fitness are always
predicates for spatially existent objects, he directly undercuts Moore's
position that they have a separate, nonphysical existence. Thus his discussion of goodness and fitness is not merely a taxonomic quibble with
Moore; his discussion serves as the basis for proving that Moore's conception of good as simple and indefinable is mistaken. By demonstrating
that goodness is a characteristic of mental states, he is establishing the
equivalent to the fact that yellow is spatially existent and, if this is the
case, he has established that it is complex and does not have an existence
as a nonnatural, Platonic entity apart from physical reality. Keynes was
trying to take the "naivety" out of Moore's realism.[22]

Keynes does not invoke the terms *Platonism* or *Platonic* in his
discussion, but rather rests content with establishing the "negative
criterion" that good always has the characteristic of being a part of a
mental state.[23] It is clear in the conclusion of the notes, however, that
he is aware of the implications of his "criterion." By denying the
nonnatural existence of something called good and by making it a
common characteristic of human mental states, he has made Moore's
idea of an objective goodness that one can directly identify a much
fuzzier concept.

---

22. This is the reason for my incredulity at O'Donnell's (1989, 13) depiction of
Keynes's work as a "refinement" of Moore's theory.
23. It is only later that Keynes (1949) explicitly refers to this fallacious element in
Moore's work as Platonism.

If the foregoing analysis is correct, it is plain that the idea and the emotion appropriate to any given sensation are partly dependent on the nature and past history of the individual who feels. This is obvious enough; we ought not all to have precisely similar states in similar physical circumstances; common sense and the commandments are agreed on that. But we can in many cases abstract that element which ought to vary from man to man.

Assuming the approximate uniformity of human organs, we can often, if we know enough, say what, from peculiar circumstances, a man *ought* to think and feel:—not indeed what he *can* think and feel—that will always depend on his nature and his past.

In accordance, therefore, with what has gone before—those objects which normally produce sensations in correspondence to which, in normal cases, a good state of mind potentially exists, are *fit*.

It will be seen that such a scheme altogether lacks the precision which a metaphysician would desire. Subjective and relative elements are introduced. But I trust that it will not conflict with its sole basis—the testimony of actual intuition and experience.[24]

This last line in particular seems a gibe at Moore's Platonic entities, for Moore contended that one knew these entities by intuition; the process of isolating simple concepts, in fact, precisely described Moore's conception of how one intuited the existence of a Platonic entity. By referring to *"actual* intuition and experience," Keynes is presumably distinguishing his own account of the concept of good and its nature from Moore's idealized conception of the "intuition" of simple entities (which Keynes had argued do not exist). Thus one is left not with an objectively determined quality "seen" through an idealized intuition, but something that involves "subjective and relative elements," because they reside in the mental states of "actual, existent" individuals, and nowhere else.[25]

Keynes's Second Conversion

What was Keynes to do with his newfound critique of Moore's work? One answer was to further elaborate his distinction between goodness and fitness. This was the project of "A Theory of Beauty," written

---

24. "Miscellanea Ethica."
25. Davis (1991a) develops the theme of the "approximate uniformity of human organs" and its possible connections to Keynes's later thought.

during September and October 1905 at the beginning of the interlude between finishing his tripos and deciding to take the civil service exams.[26] Many phrases from "Miscellanea Ethica" are lifted directly into the latter paper and the subject matter is very similar. The relevant dichotomy for the purposes of Keynes's discussion is between beauty and fitness, with the "appropriate" feeling toward a work of art being beautiful, while the work of art itself is fit. The primary difference between the essays is that while Keynes pursues some of the same questions about how different people can be taken to see the same object in a similar way (moving the question of beauty, like good, out of the realm of the objective and "introducing subjective elements" to the discussion), he does not talk directly about the issue of indefinability.

What further to do with his critique of Moore, beyond this extension to aesthetics, soon became a moot point, however, for Keynes was to abandon his critique within a matter of months and once again convert to Moorism. "Oh! I have undergone conversion. I am with Moore absolutely on all things . . ." (17 January 1906).[27] But unlike his first conversion to Moorism or his earlier rejection of Moore's ideas, this reconversion to Moorism seems to have been influenced primarily by internal factors. In part, this involved more exegesis of *Principia Ethica* and, in part, it involved reading the most recent product of Moore's exile in Edinburgh, a paper entitled "The Nature and Reality of Objects of Perception" that had been presented to the Aristotelian Society that fall.

By late December, there appeared to be a lessening in the personal hostility that Strachey and Keynes felt toward Moore, despite a suspicion that he was still aloof toward them.

Lytton Strachey to J. M. K., 19 December 1905

I saw Moore for a quarter of an hour this morning, at Crompton's, where I heard from Ainsworth that he'd be found. I tried to urge him to come to the party, but he couldn't—or wouldn't. He was closeted

---

26. This essay is deposited in file UA/23 in the Keynes Papers.

27. It is exactly at this point that Anna Carabelli's (1988) explication of Keynes's early philosophy falters. Carabelli argues that if Keynes was an adherent of Moore's naive realism (i.e., rationalism) it was only in the period from 1903 to 1906. In fact, the story at this point is quite the opposite. It is only at the end of this period that Keynes can be argued to have fully embraced Moore's naive realism. And it is clearly this commitment to Platonism that undergirds Keynes's work in his two fellowship dissertations and in *Probability*. I explain Keynes's incorporation of Platonism into his theory of probability in the following chapter. See also Bateman 1988.

with Russell, and I don't know what high argument I may have interrupted.

J. M. K. to Lytton Strachey, 20 December 1905

I shall never dare meet Moore again without the protection of Sanger or the like. He is too remote for ease or intimacy; but one could hardly treat him as a stranger.

But while there appeared to be a slight lessening of the personal hostility of only a month earlier, a real distance still obviously existed. Thus what seems to have led to Keynes's reconsideration of Moore's philosophical position was, in large part, his concern with the philosophy, per se.

Keynes's reconsideration may have initially been motivated by a vague sense that Moore's organon was too far-reaching to fall to his own attack on one element of the superstructure. In response to a report from Strachey that he had spent an afternoon with Moore (and several others) talking about Moore's Aristotelian paper, Keynes responded that he was doubtful of the ability to crack Moore altogether.

J. M. K. to Lytton Strachey, 3 January 1906

Even still the old faith is strong upon me: I am prepared to throw over all philosophy and believe every word he tells me, even the most monstrously absurd.

Besides if you believe one single article, you're probably involved in the others too.

And one hardly feels prepared to disagree with Moore on *everything*.

Whether this reconsideration is more a statement of Moore's power as a philosopher, or self-doubt about Keynes's own ability, is not clear but it seems motivated by Keynes's attitude toward Moore's *philosophy*, rather than his *personality*. It is impossible, of course, to completely disentangle Keynes's feelings for Moore's work from his perceptions of Moore's stature, and this injects a possible external element into the story.

The strongly internal nature of Keynes's second embrace of Moorism is, however, borne out in the facts of his reconversion. His reconversion actually comes in the process of a discussion about *Principia Ethica* itself.

J. M. K. to Lytton Strachey, 17 January 1906

Oh! I have undergone conversion. I am with Moore absolutely and on all things—even secondary qualities. It happened while arguing with Ernst—who has read P. E. seven times.—Something gave in my brain and I saw everything quite clearly in a flash. But as the whole thing depends on *intuiting* the Universe in a particular way—I see that now—there is no hope of converting the world except by Conversion, and that is pretty hopeless. It is not a question of argument; all depends upon a particular twist in the mind.

The internal nature of Keynes's reconversion to Moorism is further evidenced in his account of his reading of "The Nature and Reality of Objects of Perception" in March. On 15 March 1906 he writes to Strachey that "Moore has sent the proofs of his Aristotelian article to McT[aggart] and I have just got hold of them; but I've not yet read them." Then the next day he reports back to Strachey:

J. M. K. to Lytton Strachey, 16 March 1906

I have read Moore's paper and agree with every word without exception. I think the style is more marked than ever. . . . The whole thing has simply been produced by mental muscles and by keeping his nose to the stone when anyone else would have given way. . . . Lord! the distinctions.

Although Keynes had been introduced to the ideas in the paper two and one-half months earlier in his correspondence with Strachey (2 January 1906), it is obviously not his attitude about Moore (or his method) that leads Keynes to embrace Moore's position in the paper. Rather, he seems to have become convinced of Moore's argument by virtue of the argument itself.

But regardless of the exact nature of his reconversion, the most significant point of the story is his embrace of Moore's naive realism. Keynes's emphasis on the centrality of intuition to his second conversion accords with the fact that he never again returned in his early philosophical writings to the goodness/fitness distinction and never again addressed the issue of indefinability. By embracing Moorism he forsook the idea that the only simple concept in the world is existence and moved instead to the position that one can intuit any of a number of simple qualities. Indeed, during the next several months he was to make this philosophical move to intuitionism the building block of his own emerging theory of probability. Like Moore, he employed the idea that one can isolate and identify a *simple* concept and that these concepts are *indefinable* (and not parts of mental states). Thus, while it may be possible to characterize Keynes's first conversion to Moorism in 1903 as being largely of a personal character and fostered largely by his inclusion in the coterie of Apostles, this second conversion cannot satisfactorily be characterized that way. In his reconversion to Moorism Keynes was clearly swayed by Moore's philosophy and he quite clearly embraced the Platonism that undergirded that philosophy. When he said to the Apostles on 24 February 1906, "I grant with Moore that good is a simple indefinable quality which I can only identify by direct inspection—analogous to blue or beautiful . . ." he was confirming that his conversion was complete.

CHAPTER 3

Losing Faith

There is a nice irony in Keynes's use of a religious metaphor (conversion) to describe his second embrace of Moore's philosophy. Moore's work is, after all, widely taken to be one of the cornerstones of modern analytical philosophy and nowhere would one less expect to find metaphysics than in modern analytical philosophy. Conversion seems like a perfectly inapt word in this context.

The irony is perfectly understandable, however, when one considers that Keynes was embracing Moore's naive realism. As Thomas Baldwin has so nicely demonstrated, Moore in 1906 was *not* an analytical philosopher; so long as he clung to this particular form of realism and his belief in the existence of Platonic entities known through intuition, his work simply could not truly be considered to be a part of the analytic tradition.[1] Moore himself was to jettison the trappings of his early naive realism by 1910, and the Anglo-American community of analytical philosophers embraced *Principia Ethica* only after jettisoning the idea that good is a real thing that exists in a nonnatural timeless world. While much of Moore's critique of previous ethical theories was taken as seminal, no analytical philosopher could take his conception of good seriously; it was a metaphysical entity in a nonmetaphysical world.

By 1939, when Keynes read his memoir, "My Early Beliefs," to Bloomsbury, he too realized the absurdity of his early position.[2] Shorn by that time of any illusions about his youthful beliefs, he once again employed religious metaphor; in fact he characterized his early attitude about himself and the ultimate as a "religion," though, of course, he was describing the attitude he learned from Moore rather than the one he learned from his dissenting forbears.

---

1. See Baldwin 1984, 1990. Donald Gillies has made me realize that this statement is colored by the sense of analytical philosophy shared by analytical philosophers in the late twentieth century. Platonism was a part of the work of several early analytical philosophers (e.g., Frege).

2. It is an irony, as Davis (1991b, 71) points out, that Keynes embraced a position in *Probability* that Moore (and Russell) had abandoned by 1910–11.

I have called this faith a religion, and some sort of relation of neo-platonism it surely was. But we should have been very angry at the time with such a suggestion. We regarded all this as entirely rational and scientific in character. Like any other branch of science, it was nothing more than the application of logic and rational analysis to the material presented as sense-data. Our apprehension of good was exactly the same as our apprehension of green, and we purported to handle it with the same logical and analytical technique which was appropriate to the latter. Indeed we combined a dogmatic treatment as to the nature of experience with a method of handling it which was extravagantly scholastic. Russell's *Principle of Mathematics* came out in the same year as *Principia Ethica;* and the former, in spirit, furnished a method for handling the material provided by the latter.[3]

Thus, there was no irony in his description of his position as a religion: just as clearly as any form of theism, it revolved around a metaphysic of intuited, synthetic truths. Nor was there any doubt that he had thrown over his youthful Platonism as untenable.

Thus we were brought up—with Plato's absorption in the good in itself, with a scholasticism which outdid St. Thomas, in calvinistic withdrawal from the pleasures and successes of Vanity Fair, and oppressed with all the sorrows of Werther. It did not prevent us from laughing most of the time and we enjoyed supreme self-confidence, superiority and contempt towards all the rest of the unconverted world. But it was hardly a state of mind which a grown-up person in his senses could sustain literally.[4]

In the interim, however, Keynes took more than a passing fancy in Platonism. In particular, he used it as a tool for arguing against Moore's position that one is obligated to follow the general rules of right conduct, and consequently made it the foundation of his theory of probability. Not surprisingly, the embrace of such a flawed idea later led to the abandonment of the theory that had taken him so long to bring to print (15 years from 1906 to 1921, when *A Treatise on Probability* was finally published). Ultimately, however, he found it impossible to hold onto a theory built on such an insecure basis. This chapter tells the story of how that theory was built and unraveled.

---

3. Keynes 1949, 86.
4. Ibid., 91.

An Extended Embrace

To understand how Keynes came to fully embrace Moore's ideas, how he came to employ Moore's naive realism in his own philosophy, it is necessary to go back to his quarrel with Moore's position in *Principia Ethica* that one is obligated to follow general rules of conduct. In "My Early Beliefs" Keynes identifies the primary motivation behind his early work in philosophy to be "the large part played by considerations of probability in [Moore's] theory of right conduct," and this is reflected as early as 1904 in his Apostles papers.[5] This difference with Moore, which predates his differences about indefinability and the nature of good, was again at the center of his thinking at the time of his second conversion, for it was during the 1905–6 academic year, while he prepared for the civil service exams, that Keynes roughed out the ideas for the first version of his fellowship dissertation. We have no record of his thinking on probability *per se* during this year, but by October 1906, when he reported to work at the India Office, the ideas were sufficiently worked out that he was ready to put pen to paper. Thus, Keynes's conversion to Platonism and the development of his critique against Moore's argument for rules occurred almost simultaneously.[6]

When Keynes first turned to the problem of Moore's admonition to follow the general rules of right conduct, he immediately sensed that Moore was vulnerable in his use of probabilities. This might not have been the case; when Bertrand Russell addressed the inadequacy of Moore's argument in his 1904 review of *Principia Ethica*, he did not mention probability at all. And, indeed, there are several dimensions along which Moore's advocacy of rules can be attacked. But Keynes alone saw the inherently probabilistic nature of Moore's argument and its inherent weakness.

Moore's argument in favor of rules is a precursor of the more modern versions of rule utilitarianism, in that it depends on a probabilistic

---

5. O'Donnell's (1989, 108–12, 117–19, 148–54) treatment of Keynes's early concern with rules seems stilted in its grave concern with protecting Keynes from his own assertion (in "My Early Beliefs") that he was an "immoralist" in his youth. In the broad sense in which Keynes means this in the memoir (i.e., that he was not respectful of much of conventional morality in his youth) he was undoubtedly right, as the record of his youthful behavior bears out.

6. Much of what follows draws from Bateman 1988. In the first volume of Skidelsky's biography (1985) he failed to see this story clearly. In his second volume (1992) he reports the early story more accurately, but without mentioning that he had not told the same story in the earlier volume.

argument or what is now termed the expected utility (EU) model. In the case of Moore and Keynes, it is, of course, more correct to refer to the expected good (EG) model since both eschewed the idea that utility drives behavior, but this important distinction aside, the logic of Moore's position is the same as that of rule utilitarians who argue that by following rules one increases the number of times that a good outcome occurs.[7] Moore's argument was that the best course of action was the one with the highest expected (or most probable) good.

> We have, however, not only to consider the relative goodness of different effects, but also the relative probability of their being attained. A less good, that is more likely to be attained, is to be preferred to a greater, that is less probable, if the difference in probability is great enough to outweigh the difference in goodness. [8]

One must consider *both* the goodness of an action's consequences and the frequency with which they occur before deciding how to act: the correct action is then the one that has the highest valued outcomes, on average.

Moore actually felt that *full* knowledge of the probabilities needed for making EG calculations was impossible. One could not know all the possible consequences of one's actions through the infinity of time, or the relative frequencies with which different consequences would occur over such a horizon. For this reason, Moore argued that one must make an assumption that the long-run probability of "bad" results from any particular action is very small due to the intervening circumstances beyond one's control; on the basis of this assumption, one could then make short-run EG calculations over the range of time for which one did know the relative frequencies of different consequences.

It was over this shorter, knowable horizon that Moore made his argument for adhering to rules. Moore accepted that most of the rules actually adhered to in society did, in fact, generally cause the greatest good.

> It seems, then that with regard to any rule which is *generally* useful, we may assert that it ought *always* to be observed, not on the ground that in *every* particular case it will be useful, but on the

---

7. J. O. Urmson's (1970) essay is the first explicit argument that Moore's position in *Principia Ethica* is a type of rule utilitarianism. See also Baldwin 1990.

8. Moore 1903, 166.

ground that in *any* particular case the probability of its being so is greater than that of our being likely to decide rightly that we have before us an instance of its disutility. In short, though we may be sure that there are cases where the rule should be broken, we can never know which those cases are, and ought, therefore never to break it.[9]

The argument for rules is thus an argument that they represent the way of causing the greatest frequency of good outcomes.[10] This was the position that Keynes could not countenance. As he was to recollect in "My Early Beliefs" when he was describing the attitudes that character-ized the younger Apostles at the time,

We entirely repudiated a personal liability on us to obey general rules. We claimed the right to judge every individual case on its merits, and the wisdom, experience, and self-control to do so suc-cessfully. This was a very important part of our faith, violently and aggressively held, and for the outer world it was our most obvious and dangerous characteristic.[11]

Unlike the other Apostles at this time, however, who apparently chose just to ignore Moore's argument on rules, Keynes felt compelled to examine it carefully and to "disprove" it. The earliest textual evidence of Keynes's interest in the problem is in a paper he read to the Apostles on 23 January 1904, just three months after the publication of *Principia Ethica*. The paper takes its title from the fifth chapter of the book, "Ethics in Relation to Conduct," on which Moore makes his argument for following rules.[12]

---

9. Moore 1903, 162–63, italics in the original.

10. Tom Regan (1986) tries to argue that Moore was not a true proponent of rule following. As against his position, see Baldwin's (1988) critique.

11. Keynes 1949, 97.

12. This essay is now in file UA/19 of the Keynes Papers. Skidelsky (1985) was the first to provide this date for the paper. Moggridge (1992, 131–36) has disputed the date with a detailed appendix. I accept Skidelsky's dating for several reasons, Moggridge's argument notwithstanding. The first, and most persuasive, piece of evidence is a transcrip-tion of the record of the papers Keynes presented to the Apostles, which is now available in the Modern Archive, King's College, Cambridge. Although the record only records the question on which the Apostles voted after the paper was presented, and not its title, the question for 23 January 1904 ("Is there an objective probability?") would seem the obvious one to go with "Ethics in Relation to Conduct." I also find a large part of Moggridge's argument regarding the contents of this paper relative to other papers (which have undis-

Keynes's purpose in this paper was to find some way to argue against Moore's probabilistic justification for following rules. The tack he chose was to argue against Moore's use of a frequency theory of probability.

> I am not clear as to what interpretation underlies Moore's use of the word [probability]. There is, however, one view at least which does necessitate just such a proof as Moore declares to be necessary; and it is this view which I will mainly discuss.
>
> Any adequate definition of probability I have never seen, and I am unable to give one; but it is possible to try to refute given definitions and to find out the real questions at issue. It is constantly assumed that the correctness of such an assertion as "this is probably so" can be confirmed or refuted by future events. In other words it is supposed that the statement of a probability makes a prophecy of certain truths concerning events. According to this view "*x* will probably happen" means "I do not know whether *x* will happen in any particular case, but if a large number of cases be taken, I do know for certain that *x* will happen more often than not."

Probability had not been defined in *Principia Ethica,* but Keynes's characterization of Moore's implicit theory as a frequency theory was clearly correct. Moore had stated that the argument for rules was based on probability in the sense that certain rules should be followed since they result in the greatest frequency of good outcomes. Similarly, his argument against breaking these rules was based on the impossibility of knowing in which particular case the rule will fail to yield the best possible outcome.

As Keynes himself notes, his approach in this early paper is strictly critical rather than constructive. There is no evidence that he had done any reading in the topic of probability or induction at this time and he was "unable to give" any satisfactory definition to supplant Moore's

---

puted dates) to rely on an unconvincing construction. This construction is the idea that the essay contains a well-articulated theory of probability; clearly, it does not, as Keynes himself points out. If, instead, we read the paper as an early critique of Moore's use of a frequency theory that does not itself offer a clear alternative theory, the early 1904 date makes very much sense. On this reading, Keynes queried the meaning of probability three times that year in Apostles papers (in this essay and in "Toleration" and "Truth"), noted his continued interest the next year in "Miscellanea Ethica," but did not offer a theory to counter Moore's use of the frequency theory until after he had converted to Moore's naive realism in early 1906.

frequency theory. There are intimations of what he senses might be the foundation of a true theory of probability, but these are nothing more than intimations. The inchoate state of his thoughts is probably best captured in his discussion of the classical case of what it means to say "the probability of a head is one-half" when considering the outcome of a coin toss.

Surely it is plain that "heads and tails are equally probable" means simply and solely that "there is no known reason favouring either heads or tails" and that this is the meaning of the addition "if the tossing is fair." A toss is clearly fair if no party to the transaction knows of any reason favoring the fall of either heads or tails. And the interpretation that is true in this case seems to me to be equally satisfactory in the general case. A statement of probability always has reference to the available evidence and cannot be refuted or confirmed by subsequent events.

Keynes's conception here of what probability might mean clearly has to do with our knowledge about the processes involved and our best judgment of what *might* occur given this knowledge, but he denies that probability has anything to do with the *actual* outcomes. An approach such as this would seem to be dictated by the nature of Moore's argument: the frequency theory had to be denied and some alternative based on one's best estimate of the possible outcomes would have to be substituted in order to undermine Moore's argument for rules. But exactly how to conceptualize these nonfrequency probabilities still escaped Keynes.[13]

Keynes's uncertainty over how to deal with probability is apparent in two papers written later in the same year: "Truth" (October) and "Toleration" (November).[14] Both papers deal with the question of when one is bound to follow general rules (to *always* seek the truth and to *always* be tolerant) and both consider how the question of the probable outcomes of one's actions should bear on one's decisions.

The first of the papers sidesteps the issue of the meaning of probability as Keynes endorses the idea that one should follow the

---

13. It is this inability on Keynes's part to offer a clear alternative theory of probability that belies much of Moggridge's argument concerning the date of the paper. Keynes has an insight into the weakness of Moore's argument, but since he offers no well-articulated alternative theory, it is difficult (if not impossible) to compare "the theory of probability" in the paper with his later work in his dissertations.

14. Both papers are deposited in file UA/18 in the Keynes Papers.

rule of pursuing the truth. In this *apparent* turn against his own proclivity to disavow rules, Keynes relies on his faith that probable outcomes are less important in the balance than the importance of always pursuing the truth.

> I fancy we follow truth because it is truth, and not because we have justified our course by the calculus of probabilities. We do somehow believe that truth must turn out better in the end, and yet I find it difficult even to ascertain that the probabilities are in its favor, before that end, whatever it is, is reached.

This apparent disavowal of his disdain for rules must be kept in perspective, however, for the very next month Keynes repeats his oft-stated disregard for rules in general in "Toleration."

Given his absolute commitment in the first paper to seeking *true* good, Keynes uses the second paper to directly address the role of probable outcomes in this pursuit. In response to his own question, "Ought we to be tolerant always or only when it suits our purposes?" Keynes offers that any argument for intolerance must have "a vast preponderating probability" on its side. He then articulates three possible positions:

1. We should never be intolerant under any circumstances.
2. It is a "good general rule" to be tolerant, but this rule can "sometimes be cast aside after the most careful deliberations."
3. We are so incapable, by virtue of our prejudices and biases, of correctly identifying the special cases in which it would be better to be intolerant, that we are thus obligated to follow "the preponderate probability" on the side of following the rule of tolerance in all cases.

His further analysis of these three positions is telling not only because it reflects his general disdain for rule following, but because it echoes the concerns expressed earlier in January about the treatment of probability.

> The first alternative I certainly reject. I do not believe that there is any action whatever, of which it may be said without reservation or qualification that it is always to be performed. There is no action so bad in itself that its badness cannot be outweighed by the excellence of the state of affairs subsequent to and dependent upon its performance.

The second alternative seems to me to be true so far as it goes, but does it go far enough? The distinction between the third alternative and the first rests upon a subtlety which I must endeavour to make clear.

My point is this: We can never say—The performance of *x* will, on no occasion whatever, produce less good than its non-performance. But perhaps we can sometimes say: There is on all occasions *a probability* that the performance of *x* will produce less good than its non-performance: and it is probabilities that must guide our actions. This last position may or may not be true; I am not sufficiently clear about the meaning and method of determining probability. But this is an involved question, not peculiar to the principle of toleration.

So, as earlier in January, he intuits the role of probability in arguments for following rules, but falters on exactly how one might escape the frequency theory to argue against rules.[15] There is no record of Keynes's further thoughts on the meaning of probability in 1905 and we only learn of the conclusions to which he came in 1906 by way of the first draft of his fellowship dissertation, which was begun that year. There is evidence of his continuing concern with rules in his Apostles paper, "Modern Civilization," which was read in October 1905, but though he argues there that we have no duties, the argument does not involve questions of probable outcomes. In his notes, "Miscellanea Ethica," written over the long vacation of 1905, Keynes mentions "the difficult question of the probable grounds of action, and the curious connexion between 'probable' and 'ought' " but the idea is developed no further. The bulk of 1905, then, was spent in Keynes's critique of Moore's doctrine of indefinability (see chap. 2, "Examining the Indefinable") and the question of the "curious connexion" remained unanswered.

Not until the following year, when he reconverted to Moorism, does he appear to have returned with earnest to the problem of probability's definition. As it turned out, the resolution of his quandary over the meaning of probability was inexorably tied up with his reconversion; the extant documents, however, do not provide enough evidence to tell us whether his reflections on rules and probability led to his reconversion to Moorism. We do not know if his argument in January with Ernst Goldschmidt about *Principia Ethica* (see chap. 2, "Keynes's Second Conversion") was about rules and probabilities, about indefin-

---

15. Moggridge (1992, 131–36) apparently overlooks the similarity between Keynes's arguments against rules in "Ethics in Relation to Conduct" and "Toleration."

ability, or about something else altogether. Sometime during 1906, he came to advocate the position that probabilities, like good, are simple, indefinable entities. Now, instead of arguing against Platonism, he went in completely the opposite direction and defined probabilities as Platonic entities! All we know is that in the same year that he embraced Moore's naive realism he extended this embrace to encompass his conception of probability.

Rational Expectations

It was sometime, then, between his second conversion to Moorism in January 1906 and his assumption of his post at the India Office in October 1906, that Keynes came to the conclusion that probability, like good, was a Platonic entity.[16] When he reported in February 1906 in "Egoism" that he granted "with Moore that good is a simple indefinable quality which I can only identify by direct inspection—analogous to blue or beautiful" he was poised to make a similar statement about probability, if he had not already done so in his own mind. But, as he later reported in "My Early Beliefs," he was working at the time under the influence of both Moore and Russell and this is evident in his decision to term this new Platonic entity a *logical relation*. Russell was himself a Platonist at this time, and his acquiescence in Moore's Platonist project undoubtedly lent credence to it that helped make Keynes's reconversion easier; but Russell's real contribution came from his work with Alfred North Whitehead in the *Principles of Mathematics*. The effort in the *Principles* to put mathematics on a logical basis led Keynes to attempt a similar move for probability. Just as Russell and Whitehead had treated the logic of *deduction* (if p, then q), Keynes wished to treat the logic of *induction* (if p, probably q).

Labeling a probability a logical relationship thus placed Keynes in

---

16. Anna Carabelli (1988) has constructed a completely different argument about the nature of Keynes's probabilities at this time. Instead of objective, indefinable relations, she sees intersubjective probabilities based in large part on the social group(s) to which one belongs. One of her main supports for this interpretation seems to be an ahistorical reading of a term, ordinary language, that Keynes often used to defend his platonism. Keynes would often say at this time (and in *Probability*) that he was simply using words in their ordinary usage, or their usage in *ordinary language*. This specific term was later to become a moniker for the Wittgensteinian position that meaning is defined socially, by groups of people. There is no historical reason, however, to suppose that Keynes's usage, which predates the Wittgensteinian term, indicates an affinity at this time with the later usage. Keynes may have come later in his life to a position like Wittgenstein's, but that is a different story.

the mainstream of contemporary Cambridge philosophy.[17] And, like his contemporaries, he was also masking the metaphysics of his Platonism in the rhetoric of science and logic. Remember his own soft poke in 1938 at himself and his early beliefs, "We regarded all this as essentially rational and scientific in character." Keynes was working from a desire to discredit the frequency theory of probability and wished to replace it with something that allowed an agent to act in the way the agent believed was best; when someone was faced with a decision over whether to break a rule, he wanted them to be able to speak of the choice that was "probably best" without reference to what percentage of times the "best" outcome occurred. If one was to say "I am probably right to break this rule," he wanted the statement to refer to the agent's best estimate of how things would turn out in the particular case. But if this judgment of probable outcomes was to have any real warrant, if it was to rise above the level of a guess or hunch, it needed to be carefully constructed. What better warrant than to label it a "logical relation"? If the probability upon which one acts is *logical,* then one *must* be warranted in one's actions.

To better understand what it means to say that a probability is a logical relation, it is perhaps best to go back to basics and consider the ways in which probability can be defined. At first sight this may seem a daunting task. A brief review of the literature reveals a plethora of types of probability—objective, subjective, logical, rational, scientific, intuitive, type one, type two, axiomatic, personal, physical, psychological, and relative frequency, to name a few. Recently, however, Ian Hacking has proposed a simple lexicon for reclassifying these many types of probability. Because this approach clarifies the discussion, and because even those who disagree with Hacking concerning the true meaning of probability find merit in his system of distinctions,[18] it is a very helpful tool.[19] According to Hacking, there are only two basic ideas of what

---

17. It is almost undoubtedly his place in the mainstream of Cambridge philosophy that garnered his book many respectful reviews. Indeed, several of those respectful reviews were by other "Cambridge philosophers" (e.g., Broad and Russell). O'Donnell (1989, 25–27) contains a nice montage of excerpts from the reviews, though this perhaps fails to provide a full sense of the fact that despite the respectful reviews, no one actively pursued Keynes's theory of probabilities after the publication of his book. Philosophers such as H. Jeffreys, who considered themselves adherents of a logical theory of probability, explicitly rejected Keynes's arguments about measurability and were not naive realists (i.e., Platonists).

18. Kyburg (1978) is an example of someone who disagrees with Hacking's conception of probability, but accepts his two-part schema.

19. O'Donnell (1989, 23–24), on the other hand, creates a tripartite division, as opposed to Hacking's two-part schema, but his third category is redundant. What O'Donnell

probability is. One of these is the idea that the probability of an event is its long-run frequency of occurrence. Since this conception of probability is based on the proportion, percentage, or fraction of times that an event occurs in repeated trials, it is called *aleatory probability* (from a Latin word for a dice game, *alea*). The other conception of probability focuses on the uncertainty of the final outcome implicit in the idea of probability. According to this conception, a probability is the degree of belief that one has in a hypothesis, given some evidence. Because this conception depends on one's knowledge of the likelihood of a particular event, rather than solely on its relative frequency, it is called *epistemic probability* (from *episteme*, the Greek word for knowledge).

Another distinction, however, in addition to this dichotomy concerning the nature of probability, is that between objective and subjective conceptions of probability. An objective theory of probability is one in which the probabilities are unique and have the same value for all individuals with the same information. In contrast, a subjective theory of probability is one in which the probabilities take whatever value is assigned by the individual using them. In a subjective theory, two individuals with identical information could assign different values to the probability of the same proposition without either being mistaken; since all probabilities are individually determined, this result might be expected.[20]

In an objective theory, such a result would be impossible, or would indicate a mistake on the part of one of the individuals; there is only one true value for the probability of a proposition in an objective theory.

It is especially important to realize that the two types of distinction being made are not the same. An epistemic theory of probability, for instance, may be an objective or a subjective theory. Epistemic is not synonymous with subjective, nor aleatory with objective, in this lexicon. The importance of maintaining the distinction is that while many people have assumed that all epistemic theories are subjective, the theory that

---

labels as his third category is fully defined in Hacking's schema. By not recognizing the redundant nature of his third category (i.e., the logical concept), O'Donnell allows himself a false sense of distinction between the work of Keynes and Ramsey.

20. There is always the possibility, of course, that groups of people will form their probabilities according to some kind of group norm. That is, that individual members of a group (with the same information) will all share the same estimate of a probability. When probabilities are formed according to group norms, they are referred to as intersubjective probabilities. After Keynes abandoned his work in *Probability*, he embraced this idea of *intersubjectivity* and made it central to *The General Theory*. I have chosen not to label intersubjective probabilities as a separate category because I take it to be the case that in a world of subjective probabilities some individuals will form their own estimates, and some will form them on the basis of group identity.

Keynes espoused in his dissertations and in *A Treatise on Probability* was an *objective epistemic* theory. Understanding the objectivity of his early probabilities is necessary both to understanding the nature of his project and to understanding his later abandonment of the project.[21]

The nature of his original project, of course, was to construct a theory of behavior under uncertainty that sanctioned the primacy of individual judgment over conventional rules. Both drafts of the dissertation attest to this with their numerous references to the fact that the only reason that probability is worth studying is that it helps to delimit the nature of correct ethical conduct.[22] Both dissertations also explicitly debunk Moore's frequency theory as a proper guide to ethical conduct. The revolutionary step in his thinking that allowed Keynes to escape Moore's argument was the perception that the probabilities upon which we act, the "very guide of life," were *objective* degrees of belief with the status of a logical relation. Keynes refused to acknowledge that the probability of *x* could be defined by the frequency of its future (or past) occurrence. Instead, he posited that probability referred to an objective likelihood of a particular outcome, given one's evidence. In order to give such a probability the necessary warrant, it was crucial that it not be *subjective*—hence his construction of an *objective epistemic* probability, or a logical relation.

His groping toward this position is clear in both the 1907 and 1908 versions of his fellowship dissertation.[23]

The objective and logical character of probability may sometimes be lost sight of, because we are mainly interested in it for practical reasons. It is not true that probability measures the degree of belief which we do or should psychologically entertain, nor does it measure the degree of our knowledge. It is not compounded, as has often been stated, of our part knowledge and part ignorance. The relation has not necessarily anything to do either with us or

---

21. O'Donnell's (1989) inability to see that his "logical concept" of probability is synonymous with what I have here labeled an "objective epistemic" theory is where the redundancy slips into his argument.

22. There are typescripts of both of Keynes's dissertations in TP/A (first dissertation) and TP/B (second dissertation) in the Keynes Papers. Keynes's early statements about the primacy of ethical considerations to the importance of probability disappear after his work on induction. After that point he felt ethics was one of several important reasons for studying probability.

23. The following quotations are from a corrected (i.e., marked up) typescript of the dissertation submitted in 1907. This typescript was used to make the typescript of the 1908 version of the dissertation.

our knowledge. But it *is* true that its practical importance is entirely due to the fact that it is only partial knowledge which we actually do possess. Each of us has a certain body of knowledge, which for reasons good or bad, we take to be real knowledge; but we are compelled to make a vast number of judgments which, as we recognize, cannot be deduced from those propositions of which alone we are certain. Of alternative propositions, between which we must, practically, choose, we are constantly seeking to determine the probable relation to our main body of convictions. The importance of probability is this, that we judge, rightly or wrongly, that we ought to weigh alternatives according to the magnitude of the probable relation which each possesses to that body of propositions which we take to be true.[24]

Having begun by stressing the "objective and logical character" of these probable relations, Keynes goes on to reiterate that they are *not* subjective.

The purely subjective and psychological view of probability has not, so far as I know, any wholehearted adherents. It is easy enough to cite authors who have argued that probability deals with "degrees of belief"; but they usually go on to explain that they mean "degree of rational belief," "degrees of belief which ought to be held under the circumstances."[25]

This desire to construct an objective theory of epistemic probability lay at the heart of all Keynes's work in the field from 1906 to 1921. From the beginning there were several chapters devoted to the calculus of the subject and over time there was an increasing number of chapters dealing with related philosophical ideas (first the applications to ethical conduct, then to chance, cause, and induction), but throughout, objective epistemic probability lay at the heart of the project.

Not that the construction of such a theory was without problems. The first version of the dissertation was unsuccessful because of the objections of Alfred North Whitehead, one of the two readers. Whitehead's objections, which dealt largely with Keynes's treatment of the frequency theory, were addressed in the second version of the dissertation with the

---

24. Ibid., 6–8.
25. Ibid., 24.

introduction of a new chapter entitled, "The Frequency Interpretation of Probability." This replaced his more cavalier treatment in the first version, in which he had referred to Venn's work in the *Logic of Chance* as a "tissue of confusions."[26]

But even greater than his problems with providing a good critique of the frequency theory were his problems with justifying the existence of the metaphysical entities he was postulating. His own lingering sense of self-doubt is especially clear in the second version of the dissertation. It is evident even in the Introduction.

> According to the view taken in this essay the theory of probability is neither as mysterious nor as powerful as is sometimes supposed. But the fundamental difficulties to be encountered are very great, and the topics, in the treatment of which a controversial style can hardly be avoided, very numerous. The writer wishes to state here, what is not always easy to explain in the course of the discussion, the strong doubts he feels, especially in Part I, when he has attempted a constructive theory.[27]

Subtle, but clear, admissions of his self-doubt also appear elsewhere in the second dissertation.

> A successful issue of these enquiries greatly depends upon the elucidation of clearer notions than at present exist on what I have called the metaphysic of probability. We must discover, if we can, the justification of our perpetual assumptions that some propositions afford, independently of experience or demonstrative reasonings, some ground or probability in favor of others. The problems of the validity of Induction and Analogy, to which it has been possible to give no satisfactory solutions in this and the preceding chapter, do not stand alone. They are part of a general problem in the theory of knowledge which has not yet received a very close examination.[28]

But perhaps the clearest statement of the problem that Keynes saw for his theory comes in one of the early core chapters, "The Problem of Premisses in Probability treated historically." This chapter, after revision to take out the critical self-reflection, would eventually become chapter

---

26. TP/A_{1-2}, Keynes Papers, 24.
27. TP/B_1, Keynes Papers, v.
28. Ibid., 288.

4 in *Probability,* where it appears as a part of part 1 (Fundamental Ideas). In its 1908 manifestation, however, it begins by addressing the question of the ontological status (existence) of his probabilities without coming to any real resolution.

> The problem to be attacked in this Chapter must be, in a sense, the *crux* of any philosophy of probability. It is the metaphysic of the subject. Up to this point it has been assumed that knowledge concerning the probability of propositions is *possible.* It has been assumed already and it will be assumed throughout Part II, that certain probabilities are known to be equal or unequal to certain others, and the argument is concerned with the manipulation of these given quantities. *The more ultimate problem of providing the material for the logical calculus is ignored.* (Italics added.)
> There is warrant for this in the ordinary practice of logicians. The discovery of premisses they leave to the metaphysicians. Their province is to manipulate *given* premisses, and to discover what conclusions are related to these premisses by way of inference. Their logical processes cannot avoid a hypothetical element, or of themselves tell us what is true. In the same way the logic of probability cannot tell us unaided *what* is probable. It pretends only to be a method by which certain assertions of probability can be shown to be related by way of inference to certain other assertions of a similar kind. . . .
> How then do we know any probability? How are we to make any discoveries in the subject? What ground have we for any of our assertions?[29]

The chapter attempts no *direct* answer to these questions. Instead, it develops Keynes's highly regarded theory of when one knows that several different propositions have equiprobability. The implication is that if one can clearly elucidate when it is legitimate to say that several alternatives are equally likely, then one must have identified something (i.e., a probability) that actually exists.

It is easy to see the confusion in Keynes's argument; since he has started by saying that logicians simply assume the existence of probabilities to get on to the problems of the calculus, he is working on the premise that if he can provide a sufficient defense for when it is legitimate to employ a specific numerical measure for a probability, then he

---

29. Ibid., 58–59.

will have also identified (as opposed to assumed) the existence of the probabilities under consideration. But like arguments that attempt to prove the existence of God by design, Keynes's argument in the end offers no compelling proof of the existence of the thing it is meant to identify. Whereas a natural theologian looks at the wonder of the complexity of nature and argues from this complexity that it must have been created by God, Keynes looked at his proof of the conditions for equiprobability and argued that this must prove the existence of the probabilities with which he was working.

This type of indirect argument may have come to strike Keynes as unsatisfactory, for it was dropped in the revision of the chapter for *Probability*. It seems likely, however, that there was more to dropping his earlier metaphysical claims than a simple recognition that the nature of this *particular* argument was unsatisfactory, for in *Probability* the self-doubt evident in the positive construction of his theory is gone altogether. In part, this reflects the introduction to the book of two long parts on induction (parts 3 and 5) and the removal to those two parts of the difficult question of how one knows one's prior (or initial) probabilities. But it also reflects a marked change in the tone of his core chapters and introduction; no longer does he second-guess himself (or have to apologize for doing so). By 1921, the Moorean nature of his probabilities is clear and unmistakable: they are objective, indefinable, and Platonic.

In the sense important to logic, probability is not subjective. It is not, that is to say, subject to human caprice. A proposition is not probable because we think it so. When once the facts are given which determine our knowledge, what is probable or improbable in these circumstances has been fixed objectively, and is independent of our opinion.[30]

A *definition* of probability is not possible, unless it contents us to define degrees of the probability-relation by reference to degrees of rational belief. We cannot analyze the probability-relation in terms of simpler ideas.[31]

What is more, in the peculiar sense of Cambridge philosophy in the first decade of the twentieth century, these probabilities are also "ra-

---

30. Keynes 1921, 4. See also the paean to Moore's "style" in chapter 2 of *Probability* (ibid., 19).
31. Ibid., 8.

tional." Just as Moore assumed that rationality was defined by acting so as to achieve the good, Keynes assumed that acting in accordance with his probabilities (acting so as to achieve the *most probable* good) represented rational behavior. For Moore, Russell, and Keynes, rationality was defined in the context of acting in accord with the true, Platonic entities. In this sense, rational expectations would be those formed as the result of intuiting, or cognizing, these Platonic entities and allowing them to dictate one's behavior.

While there does not appear to be extant evidence that explains Keynes's growing self-assurance as regarded the existence of his Platonic logical relations, it is clear that their rational status aided him in developing the argument that supplanted his self-doubt. In addition, by the time he published *Probability* he had fully developed a concept of *unknown probabilities* and insisted that these represented a case in which people simply lacked the logical ability or rationality to see what was there. "The theory of probability is logical, therefore, because it is concerned with the degree of belief which it is *rational* to entertain in given conditions, and not merely with the actual beliefs of particular individuals, which may or may not be rational."[32]

> To say, then, that a probability is unknown ought to mean that it is unknown to us through our lack of skill in arguing from given evidence. The evidence justifies a certain degree of knowledge, but the weakness of our reasoning power prevents our knowing what this degree is. At the best, in such cases, we only know *vaguely* with what degree of probability the premises invest the conclusion. The probabilities can be unknown in this sense or known with less distinctness than the argument justifies, is clearly the case. We can through stupidity fail to make any estimate of a probability at all, just as we may through the same cause estimate a probability wrongly. As soon as we distinguish between the degree of belief which it is rational to entertain and the degree of belief actually entertained, we have in effect admitted that the true probability is *not* known to everybody.[33]

Keynes goes on to indicate that he does not mean by this that there is widespread irrationality, or that he assumes "perfect logical insight" on the part of everyone, but his implication is clear: not everyone has

---

32. Ibid., 4.
33. Ibid., 32.

what it takes to know probabilities, and we should not be surprised that they do not.[34]

Rejecting Platonism

For those people lucky enough to possess the logical insight to know, or intuit, probabilities, the question of their responsibility to follow the rules of conventional behavior appeared to be answered. Employing their knowledge of the good that would attach to each possible outcome of an action, together with the probability of each of these possible outcomes, it would be possible to make expected good (EG) calculations that revealed the probable goodness of the action. "Rational" people would then choose the action with the highest expected good.

This conclusion marked the triumph of individual judgment over rules, at least in the sense in which Moore had argued for following rules. By displacing Moore's frequency theory of probability with his own logical theory, Keynes removed the basis for Moore's argument that one should take the action with the highest frequency of good outcomes. No longer was it necessary to argue over which instances of an action would have good outcomes and which would have bad outcomes; probability was not about frequencies anymore. In its place he offered the doctrine that one should intuit the objective probability of each outcome and act on this intuition. Keynes addresses this application of his ideas in chapter 26 of *Probability,* a chapter that originated in his 1907 dissertation and that survived intact through all three versions of the work. In particular, Keynes attacks Moore's use of a frequency theory and his argument that the inability to know long-run frequencies obliges one to rely on the probabilities implicit in the rules of conventional behavior. It must have been a particularly gratifying triumph to have beaten Moore at his own game; using the Moorean construction of indefinability and Platonic entities to dislodge Moore's argument for rules was, after all, a neat trick.

---

34. O'Donnell (1989) has tried to make the existence of unknown probabilities the basis for arguing that Keynes never abandoned his original theory of probability. On this reading, Keynes merely came to realize that more and more probabilities were unknown and fewer and fewer people had the ability to recognize them. There are at least two problems with this interpretation. One is that it neglects the fact that Keynes's use of unknown probabilities was an unsatisfactory move in the first place that betrayed the unsatisfactory nature of his larger theory. The second is that Ramsey's (1931) critique of Keynes's original theory is directly aimed at this awkward construction (i.e., unknown probabilities) and it is this part of Ramsey's critique to which Keynes refers in his capitulation.

In his *Principia Ethica* (p. 152) Dr. Moore argues that "the first difficulty in the way of establishing a probability that one course of action will give a better total result than another, lies in the fact that we have to take account of the effects of both throughout an infinite future. . . . We must, therefore, certainly have some reason to believe that no consequences of our action in a further future will generally be such as to reverse the balance of good that is probable in the future which we can foresee. This large postulate must be made, if we are ever to assert that the results of one action will be even probably better than those of another. Our utter ignorance of the far future gives us no justification for saying that it is even probably right to choose the greater good within the region over which a probable forecast may extend."

This argument seems to be invalid and to depend on a wrong philosophical interpretation of probability. Mr. Moore's reasoning endeavours to show that there is not even a *probability* by showing that there is not a *certainty*. We must not, of course, have reason to believe that remote consequences will *generally* be such as to reverse the balance of immediate good. But we need not be certain that the opposite is the case. If good is additive, if we have reason to think that of two actions one produces more good than the other in the near future, and if we have no means of discriminating between their results in the distant future, then by what seems a legitimate application of the principle of indifference we may suppose that there is a probability in favour of the former action. Mr. Moore's argument must be derived from the empirical or frequency theory of probability, according to which we must know for certain what will happen *generally* (whatever that may mean) before we can assert a probability.

The results of our endeavours are very uncertain, but we have a genuine probability, even when the evidence upon which it is founded is slight.[35]

Keynes's argument does not end here, however. Rather than arguing that he has made the problem of rational conduct completely tractable in the guise of mathematical expectation or the simple multiplication of good and probability, he goes on to point out that there are other aspects of rational conduct. Although he felt he had found an effective counter to Moore's argument for rules, and was willing to conclude with

---

35. Keynes 1921a, 309–10.

Bishop Butler that probability was the "guide of life," he had also come to the conclusion that there were other dimensions to the problem of ethical behavior.

One of the new difficulties involved the question of the measurability of probability; Keynes had argued earlier in the book that only a very limited class of probabilities were measurable, or numerical, and this made the possibility of simple calculations of correct behavior problematic. This gave rise to his oft-quoted disclaimer regarding the usefulness of mathematics in the moral sciences.

The hope, which sustained many investigators in the course of the nineteenth century, of gradually bringing the moral sciences under the sway of mathematical reasoning, steadily recedes—if we mean, as they meant, by mathematics the introduction of precise numerical methods. The old assumptions, that all quantity is numerical and that all quantitative characteristics are additive, can be no longer sustained. Mathematical reasoning now appears as an aid in its symbolic rather than in its numerical character. I, at any rate, have not the same lively hope as Condorcet, or even as Edgeworth, "éclairer les Sciences morales et politiques par le flambeau de l'Algèbre." In the present case, even if we are able to range goods in order of magnitude, and also their probabilities in order of magnitude, yet it does not follow that we can range the products composed of each good and its corresponding probability in this order.[36]

But while the poetry of Keynes's passage has made good grist for the scholarly mill, this aspect may have been the least serious of his reservations, for he says elsewhere in *Probability* that many types of probable outcomes are estimable within narrow enough bounds to make it possible for making reasonable calculations for insurance purposes.[37]

The two other dimensions of difficulty for Keynes were what he termed *weight* and *risk*. By weight, Keynes meant the amount of confidence or credence one could place on the probabilities one employed.[38]

---

36. Ibid., 316.

37. Chapter 4 contains a discussion of contemporaneous treatments in Keynes's economics where he treats probabilities as being numerically determinant enough to allow widespread calculations based upon them.

38. Jochen Runde (1990) takes Keynes's use of weight in *The General Theory* (in a footnote) as evidence that Keynes's ideas on probability were unchanged after probability. This is not a strong argument, however, for weight, like probability, is defined as a Platonic entity in *Probability* and so by Rundes's criterion Keynes's continued use of the word

One might, for instance, intuit the correct probabilities, given one's knowledge, but if one's knowledge was slight, one might wish to gain more knowledge so that one felt more confidence in the probabilities. By risk, Keynes meant the size of the expected bad (or loss) that might occur if things went wrong. He was concerned that if there was the probability of a bad outcome, then it was not clear how to weigh this risk against the possibility of a good outcome; he felt certain that simple mathematical expectation did not adequately determine how to weigh such problems.

Like his argument against rules, the development of this more complex theory of rational behavior had a very Moorean tone. Moore was extremely averse to the idea that ethical problems were mathematically tractable and Keynes clearly reflected this bias. In addition, Keynes formulated both weight and risk as Platonic entities. Thus, although Keynes offered a complicated formula to account for probability, weight, and risk taken together, he immediately disclaimed any practical value for it and suggested that it was useful only as a heuristic.[39] One was thus left with rational individuals, who intuit all these dimensions of a problem (good, probability, weight, and risk), but not in any easily mensurable way. The sum effect, however, was to further warrant individual judgment, for there were now so many dimensions to the problem of how to act that no rule could possibly supplant the need to consider these many dimensions in any particular case. Using a full extension of Moore's Platonism, Keynes had ultimately been able to resolve the conflict in *Principia Ethica* over individual judgment versus rules in favor of individual judgment.

It is difficult to judge the "success" of Keynes's argument against following rules, since there is virtually no record of interest in it among ethical philosophers. In fact, the only place that one can possibly trace any influence is in a short popularization of his ideas that Moore himself published in 1912 entitled *Ethics*. Moore completely drops his argument for following rules in this book, but it seems much more likely to have

---

probability after his capitulation to Ramsey would also indicate that he had not changed his mind. The problem, of course, is that while Keynes abandoned his Platonism and so the idea that probabilities (and weights) are objective, this does not mean that he abandoned the idea that these words have a useful meaning in describing some aspect of human behavior. In particular, he advocated a subjective theory of probability (and weight) after his capitulation to Ramsey. But this advocacy, of course, cannot be taken to mean that he had not rejected his earlier beliefs; these were new beliefs that replaced his earlier ones.

39. Thus, Michael Brady's (1993) recent attempt to resurrect Keynes's formula is an interesting exercise in decision theory, but is ahistorical as regards Keynes.

been the force of Bertrand Russell's published criticism of *Principia Ethica* than Keynes's own nascent arguments that brought about this change. We know from Moore's diaries both that he read some of Keynes's work in the interim period between publication of his first two books and also that the two had many discussions during this period, some of which explicitly involved probability, but the degree of Keynes's direct influence on Moore's decision to drop his advocacy of rules is unclear.[40] Since Moore completely altered his use of the word *probability* in the second book to make it compatible with the sense of a logical degree of belief that Keynes had adopted in his two dissertations, it is not unreasonable to assume that Keynes's critique had *some* influence on Moore's changed position; but the greater impetus to change most probably came from Russell, given his stature at the time.[41]

It is easier to judge the "success" of Keynes's theory of probability. Although the book is widely referenced, it has been little read and has had little impact since its publication beyond the spur it provided to the alternative theories of probability offered by Frank Ramsey (1931) and Karl Popper ([1934] 1959).[42] Others in the field who take the tack of calling a probability a logical relation have never been willing to accept Keynes's idea that probabilities are not numerical. More to the point, no one in the field would adapt his Platonic metaphysics; the metaphysical aspect of his theory may well explain why the early positivists and members of the Vienna Circle never seriously considered his work as a part of their own tradition and thereby limited its importance in subsequent decades.[43]

The real blow to the success of Keynes's early work in probability, however, was that Frank Ramsey, one of the fathers of the modern subjectivist theory of probability, built his theory on a devastating critique of Keynes's work.[44] In fact, the critique was so devastating that

---

40. Moore's diaries are deposited in Box 8 of the G. E. Moore Papers, University Library, Cambridge. It is interesting to note in Moore's diaries and papers that he seems to have enjoyed Ralph Hawtrey's company much more than Keynes's.
41. In Bateman 1988 I attributed the influence solely to Keynes without considering Russell's contemporaneous critique. Tom Baldwin pointed out my probable error as regards the balance of influence.
42. O'Donnell (1989) takes the many respectful reviews of *Probability* to mean widespread interest in the book, but it is difficult to find evidence of any lasting, positive influence beyond the reviews.
43. See Bateman 1991c.
44. Bruno De Finetti's work on subjective probability was done in the 1930s independently of Ramsey's. See Gillies and Ietto-Gillies 1987 for a nice explication of De Finetti's work with a bibliography of the relevant works.

Keynes himself capitulated to Ramsey and accepted his argument that in the moral sciences we deal with subjective epistemic probabilities rather than objective ones.

Not surprisingly, Ramsey was also a Cambridge philosopher, and his critique of Keynes's theory came by way of an intimate knowledge of it. Ramsey was an active Apostle from 1921 to 1925 and he and Richard Braithwaite were the mainstays of the group during those years. Although this group of young men put the Apostles on a completely new footing, they maintained the tradition of building upon the work of their predecessors. Their predecessors, likewise, maintained the tradition of keeping up with what the active brothers were doing. Keynes, for instance, attended 27 meetings of the Apostles between 1921 and 1925 and was present at five of the seven papers that Ramsey gave to the Society. One of the papers that Keynes heard Ramsey deliver, on 20 October 1923, was a comparison of his own theory of induction with Wittgenstein's.

By this time, Ramsey's differences with Keynes were well rehearsed. In January 1922 Ramsey had published a review of *Probability* in the *Cambridge Magazine* in which he attacked Keynes's idea that probabilities are not measurable and this review foreshadows his later criticism when it likens immeasurable probabilities to mountains shrouded in mist. A recent criticism of this review by D. E. Watt derides Ramsey for not understanding more recent, rigorous proofs of the immeasurability of probability, but the criticism misses the point completely.[45] Keynes's argument for immensurability was really an *assumption* that followed from his aping of Moore's Platonism, and Ramsey was poking fun at the inadequate basis of Keynes's assertion.[46] Moore had assumed that goodness was immeasurable because of its Platonic nature, and Keynes's argument followed the same line of reasoning; Ramsey's metaphor of a mountain shrouded in mist is really no more than a gibe at the naive realism embodied in an argument of this type.

An interesting three-sided correspondence took place at this time between Keynes, Ramsey, and C. D. Broad, another Cambridge-

---

45. D. E. Watt (1989) seems to lack any understanding of the historical context of Ramsey's critique(s) of Keynes's work.

46. Ramsey might well have pointed to the awkward nature of his assumptions about measurability by comparing Keynes's Moorean statements in *Probability* with his other statements there that probabilities can be estimated within narrow enough bounds for purposes of selling insurance.

trained philosopher who had recently taken a chair at Bristol.[47] From the parts of the correspondence that exist, it is clear that Broad was involved in trying to convince Keynes of a mistake in *Probability* and Keynes was, in turn, relying on Ramsey to check through the mathematics of Broad's argument. There is a fine irony in this, for Broad was in general sympathy with Keynes's logical theory of probability, whereas Ramsey was not; still Ramsey found the mistake in Broad's calculations that appears to have put the issue to rest. The interesting thing about the correspondence is what it reveals about Ramsey's and Keynes's attitudes at the time, for Ramsey had apparently already conceived much more of his alternative to Keynes's theory than is evident in the 1922 review and Keynes knew it.

J. M. K. to C. D. Broad 31 January 1922

But what I really attach importance to is, of course, the general philosophical theory. I am much comforted that with that you are in general agreement. But I find that Ramsey and other young men at Cambridge are quite obdurate, and still believe that *either* Probability is a definitely measurable entity, probably connected with Frequency, *or* is of merely psychological importance and is definitely non-logical. I recognize that they can raise some very damaging criticism against me on these lines. But all the same I feel great confidence that they are wrong.[48]

Ramsey, in his review, had criticized Keynes's idea of the nonnumerical nature of most probabilities and had questioned whether in certain special cases it was correct to assume that a logical relation existed between two propositions (e.g., is there any probability of "my carpet is blue" given that "Napoleon was a great general"?); but he had *not* explicitly questioned the more fundamental idea that logical relations of probability exist at all. As Keynes's letter to Broad indicates, however, Ramsey had already called the very existence of these logical relations into question. One of Ramsey's letters to Keynes in this exchange further establishes the well-developed state of his argument that individual psychology, rather than logical relations, lie behind the true meaning of probability.

---

47. What appear to be all the sides to this correspondence are extant (in original or carbon copy) in the Keynes Papers.

48. This letter is in file TP/1$_1$ in the Keynes Papers.

Frank Ramsey to J. M. K. 2 February 1922

Suppose that Fermat died having asserted 6 mathematical proposition without proof; of which 5 had been subsequently proved but the sixth, say q, was doubtful. Then whatever h is, q/h = 1 or 0; but the probability

$$\left\{ \frac{\text{The only one of Fermat's props still unproved is true}}{\text{His five others have been proved, etc.}} \right\}$$

would be between 0 and 1. Supposing, that is, the evidence does not contain the statement that the prop in question is q.

That, I think, is the probability we are obliged to consider when through lack of mathematical ability we cannot perceive the logical relations of q itself. If like me, you do not know what Fermat's Last Theorem is, it is the only probability you can consider; if you do know it, it seems to me the part of the evidence which you must neglect because you cannot see its bearing. . . .

In general,

Let p be a mathematical proposition of whose truth or falsity I am ignorant. Let $\varphi(p)$ be my total knowledge about p, except p = p. Then I do not know the value of

$$\frac{P}{\varphi(p)} = \frac{x \text{ is true}}{\varphi(x) \,.\, x = p} \qquad (0 = 1)$$

and so have to disregard the evidence x = p and consider

$$\frac{x \text{ is true}}{\varphi(x)}$$

instead. {I believe "p" and "p is true" are identical} i.e., consider the probability of the truth of a random number of the class defined by φ.

This account seems to me more plausible psychologically than yours. . . . [49]

The question of "psychological plausibility" was to continue at the heart of Ramsey's critique over the next four years. The cul-

---

49. This letter is in file $TP/1_1$ in the Keynes Papers.

mination of his work was the classic essay, "Truth and Probability" (1926), in which he both laid the foundation for the modern subjectivist theory of probability and devastated Keynes's objective theory.[50] There is actually more to the story of Ramsey's work in probability than this essay on subjectivist theory, for he believed that there were both epistemic and aleatory probabilities and that advocacy of one theory did not preclude the possibility of advocating the other; his work on aleatory probability remained unfinished at his death in 1930, however, and is only now being prepared for publication.[51] His work in *aleatory* probability aside, then, the crux of his work on *epistemic* probability was his claim that one's degrees of belief are subjectively determined and have no reference to logical relations or any other objective entity. Whereas Keynes had been able to say in 1908 that "The purely subjective and psychological view of probability has not, so far as I know, any wholehearted adherents," he was now faced with the reality of a skeptic at close quarters.

Mr. Keynes starts from the supposition that we make probable inferences for which we claim objective validity; we proceed from full belief in one proposition to partial belief in another, and we claim that this procedure is objectively right, so that if another man in similar circumstances entertained a different degree of belief, he would be wrong in doing so. Mr. Keynes accounts for this by supposing that between any two propositions, taken as premiss and conclusion, there holds one and only one relation of a certain sort called probability relations; and that if, in any given case, the relation is that of degree α, from full belief in the premiss, we should, if we were rational, proceed to a belief of degree α, in the conclusion.[52]

But Ramsey would have none of it.

A . . . fundamental criticism of Mr. Keynes' views, is the obvious one that there really do not seem to be any such things as the probability relations he describes. He supposes that, at any rate in

---

50. The essay was completed in 1926 but not published until 1931.
51. The original of the draft essay on aleatory probability is deposited in the Ramsey Papers at the University of Pittsburgh.
52. Ramsey 1931, 160.

certain cases, they can be perceived; but speaking for myself I feel confident that this is not true. I do not perceive them, and if I am to be persuaded that they exist it must be by argument; moreover I shrewdly suspect that others do not perceive them either, because they are able to come to so very little agreement as to which of them relates any two given propositions.[53]

Although Ramsey's essay was not published until 1931, Keynes was well acquainted with its argument when it was completed in 1926. Keynes and Ramsey were close acquaintances by this time, not only through Keynes's continued interest in the Apostles, but through Keynes's sponsorship of Ramsey for a special fellowship in King's College. Keynes's familiarity with Ramsey's argument, and his realization of the problems it posed for his own theory, are already apparent in 1926 in his correspondence with F. M. Urban, the German translator of *Probability*.

J. M. K. to F. M. Urban 15 May 1926

I have not thought about the subject very deeply in recent times. But as time goes on I myself feel that there is a great deal in the book which is unsatisfactory, and, indeed, I felt this even when I was writing it. It was published as it stood because it seemed to me that it would help on the subject that I should do so more effectively than if I was to try to make further refinements and revisions which might quite likely prove beyond my capacity. I believe that the ultimate theory of the subject may differ considerably from mine. But I still think that the problems as I have posed them may be the right starting point for further research.

Amongst those students in England for whose opinion I feel most respect I find a marked reluctance against abandoning some variant of the frequency theory. They admit that my criticisms hold good on existing versions, and they are not yet ready to prepare a version which can resist them. But they maintain all the same that they have a strong instinct that some kind of frequency theory will be found in the end to be more fundamental to the whole conception of probability than I have yet allowed. I shall not be surprised if they prove right. I suspect, however, that the first step forward will come through progress being made with the partly psychological subject of vague knowl-

---

53. Ibid., 161.

edge, and that further developments in a strictly logical field must wait for a clear distinction between logical probability proper and the theory of what I have called vague knowledge.[54]

The last paragraph of this letter seems a virtual progress report on Ramsey's project at the time: the work on aleatory probability was unfinished, but his subjective epistemic theory was clearly articulated and marked "the first step" in the dismantling of Keynes's own theory. But while Keynes may have held onto a thread of hope of salvaging some of his own framework in 1926, as is evidenced by his use of the term *vague knowledge,* all such pretense was dropped by 1931, when Ramsey's essay was published. The concept of vague knowledge in *Probability* referred to a situation in which one imperfectly intuits a logical relation, but may be helped to "see" it through the aid of argument; in his review of Ramsey's work in 1931, Keynes finally admits there simply is not anything there to know—vaguely or otherwise.

Ramsey argues, as against the view which I had put forward, that probability is concerned not with objective relations between propositions but (in some sense) with degrees of belief, and he succeeds in showing that the calculus of probabilities simply amounts to a set of rules for ensuring that the system of degrees of belief which we hold shall be a consistent system. Thus the calculus of probabilities belongs to formal logic. But the basis of our degrees of belief—or the *a priori* probabilities, as they used to be called—is part of our human outfit, perhaps given us merely by natural selection, analogous to our perceptions and our memories rather than to formal logic. So far I yield to Ramsey— I think he is right.[55]

In the language of external and internal influences, this capitulation to Ramsey seems to be primarily an internal turn in Keynes's argument. But it is impossible to know the full impact of their close friendship and extensive personal contact. Was Keynes ultimately persuaded to change his mind by virtue of Ramsey's argument or by virtue of his personal influence? Faced with a direct challenge to the metaphysical naivety of his earlier position, Keynes seems to have

---

54. This letter is deposited in file TP/1$_2$ in the Keynes Papers.
55. Keynes 1931b, 407.

been forced into a retreat that is most clearly understood in internal-ist terms. But many people had already made sound criticisms of Keynes's theory and none of them had cracked Keynes's protective shell.

Two Treatises, Two Failures

Keynes scholars have always seen 1931 as a difficult year for him. After six years of work, he had published his *Treatise on Money* in 1930; by 1931 he was already forced to admit that his herculean effort was a failure. How much more bitter must it have been that his other *Treatise*, which had been 15 years in the making, was also a failure? Two treatises, 21 years of work, and still nothing matching the definitive status con-noted by the word *treatise*.

In reality, of course, his failure with the first *Treatise* did not have the immediacy of his failure with the second one. As his letter to Urban in 1926 reveals, it seemed altogether likely to him even then that Ram-sey would ultimately carry the day. The fall of the first *Treatise* was a gradual letdown.

But if his failure with the second *Treatise* was more immediate, neither was it completely devastating. By this time, he had finished his work with the Macmillan Committee and was a member of the Eco-nomic Advisory Council (E.A.C.), and this official work helped to shape his response to his failure. Although he was not happy that he had failed with the second *Treatise,* his failure only intensified his resolve to "get it right." At first this resolve was reinforced by his desire to use his potential to directly affect policy; this sanguine attitude lasted until the publication of "The Means to Prosperity" (1933b), in which he em-ployed the nascent concept of the multiplier to argue for more public works expenditure.

The failure of "The Means to Prosperity" seems to have marked a turning point for Keynes, however. His work on *The General Theory* had been different than his work on the *Treatise* from the beginning, in that it was done largely in the context of Cambridge rather than "in public." Whereas the argument in the *Treatise* had been developed, in part, in months of testimony before the Macmillan Committee and in the subcommittees of the E.A.C., *The General Theory* was developed "out of sight" in Cambridge in an effort to protect the theoretical devel-opment from the exigencies of public debate. But with the failure of "The Means" there was an even more profound change in Keynes's work. Part of this change was a withdrawal from his public role as a policy advocate. Peter Clarke has documented this shift away from active policy debate very well.

Another change in 1933 was the full-scale introduction of uncertainty and expectations to the model that Keynes was building. The fact that his concern with uncertainty did not surface until two years after he had formally adopted a subjective epistemic theory of probability suggests that his capitulation to Ramsey was not the immediate cause of his introduction of expectations, and that is, indeed, the case. His successes and failures with applying economic theory to policy making ultimately determined his concern with uncertainty in the *General Theory,* although the theory of expectations he ultimately applied was based on the subjective epistemic probabilities he had come to embrace in 1931.

But all of this is putting the cart before the horse. Keynes had been interested in the role of uncertainty and instability in economics from at least 1910 and had made policy recommendations based on changing expectations as early as 1910. Thus, a full telling of the story of how uncertainty functioned in Keynes's economic work must go back far before 1931 and explain his earlier concerns and how these may have led to his later position. The story of how his changing ideas about probability affected his economics must be set against a backdrop of his changing economic ideas.

Only then is it possible to satisfactorily solve das Maynard Keynes problem. If one simply looks at the succession of models of expectations and uncertainty, one does not see the full story. One can easily trace his changes of heart regarding the objectivity and rationality of expectations in his capitulation to Ramsey. But that capitulation alone does not tell the complete story of how his new ideas became embedded in his economics.

Part 3
Probability and Economics

Prologue to Part 3

After Keynes's capitulation to Ramsey in 1931, one might suppose that it was an obvious step to incorporate subjective probabilities into his economics. This was certainly my own belief when I first worked out the story of Keynes's change of heart. After all, the timing seems almost perfect: just at the moment that the Cambridge Circus convinced Keynes that he needed to scrap the *Treatise on Money,* he was also publicly admitting that a subjective theory of probability was superior to his own earlier efforts at an objective theory. It seems one easy step to see Keynes beginning work on his new theory of effective demand with his new theory of subjective probability fresh to hand. Seen in this light, it is not difficult to imagine Keynes working out the importance of uncertainty and confidence as a part of discovering *The General Theory.*

The historical reality is considerably different, however. In 1931, Keynes was involved in an argument (on many fronts) that uncertainty and business confidence were not central to an explanation of the Slump. Likewise, he denied that they were important to a theory of the capitalist economy or to policies to combat the Slump. In 1931 and 1932, Keynes expanded on some of his insights from *A Treatise on Money,* particularly as regards financial markets, but the introduction of uncertainty across the whole model did not come until late 1933. His Michaelmas lectures that year also contain his first explicit statements of the systematic importance of uncertainty to his project.

The story of how uncertainty and expectations came into *The General Theory* is even more complex, however, than tracing out Keynes's immediate reluctance to incorporate his new ideas into his evolving economic ideas. There is an added layer of complexity in the fact that earlier in his career Keynes had been an adherent of the Cambridge theory of the trade cycle, a theory that explicitly ties the trade cycle to businessmen's expectations. Thus, the last part of the story of how the author of *Probability* could also have authored *The General Theory* lies in examining how Keynes's ideas about the role of uncertainty in economic behavior changed through time. That is to say, one cannot solve das Maynard Keynes problem just by looking at his philosophical ideas.

CHAPTER 4

Confidence Lost

By the time Keynes abandoned the *Treatise on Money,* he was so deeply ensconced in contemporary debates over British economic policy that it is almost impossible to imagine his theoretical work in isolation from the influences of policy. His joint concern with theory and policy is commonplace in Keynes scholarship and is made explicit in the widespread belief that he wrote *The General Theory* primarily as a theoretical justification for public works and deficit spending. And yet, something seems wrong in this picture: scholars have come more and more to notice that *The General Theory* is bereft of almost any mention of the policies that might follow from the theory.[1] If this is a book defending government spending as a way out of the Great Depression, where is the thrust and play of the typical Keynes polemic? Where is the polished invective of the man who wrote *The Economic Consequences of the Peace* or the man who co-authored the famous election pamphlet, *Can Lloyd George Do It?*

Keynes begins *The General Theory* by saying that, "This book is chiefly addressed to my fellow economists. I hope it will be intelligible to others. But its main purpose is to deal with difficult questions of theory, and only in the second place with the applications of this theory to practice." But it is not policy to which he turns after the "difficult" task of developing his theory, at least not *fiscal* policy. Although Keynes discusses the limits inherent in monetary policy, what he really does with his theory is to show how it can be used to explain the cyclical nature of a capitalist economy. Thus it is description and explanation, rather than policy, that really comes in the "second place."

Peter Clarke has employed the internalist/externalist framework to explain this apparent shift in Keynes's approach in *The General Theory.* "While the writing of the *Treatise* can, in important respects, be explained along 'externalist' lines, by invoking the political context in which it was conceived, the composition of the *General Theory* must, in

---

1. See, for instance, Richard Kahn 1984, 158, Allan Meltzer 1988, and George Peden 1988, 38.

essentials, be understood in 'internalist' terms. It was the outcome of a process of intellectual discovery rather than of political invention."[2] This approach to the construction of Keynes's magnum opus is attractive, for it helps to identify an important difference between the construction of the *Tract* and the *Treatise,* on the one hand, and the *General Theory,* on the other. Whereas Keynes was intimately concerned with particular policy questions in the construction of the first two books, and composed them in an almost public manner, his last book was constructed in the relatively quiet retreat of Cambridge, away from particular policy debates, and with a decided eye to theoretical triumph.

This change in approach arose in part, as Clarke suggests, because Keynes saw his efforts to construct the *Treatise* for use as a debating tool in the Macmillan Committee as having had a detrimental effect on its integrity as a theoretical work. The potential for problems in this regard was already evident in a letter to his mother written on the day that he finished the book: "Artistically it is a failure—I have changed my mind too much during the course of it for it to be a proper unity." As the negative reviews rolled in, this self-awareness must have become more acute.[3] His many efforts to change the direction of his argument in order to make the *Treatise* fit the exigencies of an ongoing policy debate had undoubtedly lent to its uneven quality and to the holes in the theoretical argument. In this sense, it seems clear that Keynes was personally dissatisfied with the large external influence in the composition of the *Treatise.*

But Keynes was not only frustrated by external intrusions on his theoretical work. There were also internal problems with the *Treatise.* The initial impetus to throw over the book was the *internal* consideration that it assumed that output and employment were fixed in the long run and provided no model for how they fluctuated in the short run. This flaw in his model was first worked out in the vaunted Circus in 1931, and led him in quick succession in 1932 to develop his theories of the consumption function, effective demand, and liquidity preference. Formally, this left him only one step from his full-blown model in *The General Theory;* all that was missing was the theory of the marginal efficiency of capital. But even after addressing the problem of how to model changes in output there was still another important internal problem with Keynes's work at this time, for he continued to work in the same theoretical mindset that had characterized his work in the *Treatise:*

---

2. Clarke 1988, 230.

3. Keynes's letter to his mother is dated 14 September 1930. It is reproduced (in part) at page 176 in *JMK,* xiii. The *Treatise on Money* appeared on 31 October 1930.

he still employed the "magic formula mentality," or the belief in the efficacy and power of a particular algebraic construct.

Don Patinkin was the first to point out this aspect of Keynes's thought in the *Treatise,* and likewise the first to point out its deleterious effect on Keynes's work as a theorist.[4] When one has a magic formula, one does not easily see the limitations and problems inherent in the overall structure of one's work. But in early 1933, when Keynes published *The Means to Prosperity,* he was still in the thrall of this limiting mentality. Now instead of his "Fundamental Equations," he had the nascent version of his multiplier theory, but the mindset was the same: this formula, this *simple* formula, shows us the road to recovery! Not until Keynes had shed this naive scientism would he finally achieve the integration of his new tools into a general theory.

It is at this decidedly internal juncture of the story that an important external element reentered the picture: his failure at influencing policy. On the simplest level, this consisted of the recognition that his work in the *Treatise* had not been persuasive. Despite sitting on the two newly created government committees for soliciting expert economic opinion; despite his position as Britain's leading economic journalist; despite his ability to gain direct access to any official; and, most of all, despite his two-volume *Treatise,* Keynes's arguments about policy were still not carrying the day. This external, political failure must have helped to make him more receptive to the internal weaknesses in his theory. The holes in his argument left too many openings to his critics for the work to have the compelling force that he had hoped for it.

More importantly, however, his many debates about policy between 1930 and 1933 often came back to an element that Keynes refused to take seriously: business confidence. Not until 1933 did Keynes finally take this element of his opponents' arguments seriously and give it recognition as a necessary part of his own theory. This recognition sparked the development of the fourth and final part of his general theory, the marginal efficiency of capital, the part that he said "linked up" the other

---

4. See Patinkin 1976, 53, 126. The phrase is a particularly apt one because it so closely echoes Keynes's own discussion in chapter 37 of the *Treatise* in which Keynes first quotes from Benjamin Strong regarding Strong's doubt that "the Federal Reserve System has the power to raise or lower the price-level by some automatic method, by some magical mathematical formula," and then goes on to admit that Strong's concern cannot be addressed "merely by pointing to the truism of a Quantity Equation" (1930, vol. 2, 340, 345). Keynes was clearly guilty in the *Treatise* of arguing from this "truism," despite his disclaimer. Clarke (1988, 313) refers to this same bent in Keynes's thinking by reference to his "magic tool kit."

three components and made them a whole. Thus it was that the development of *The General Theory* was to have an important externalist dimension. Before the fact, there was no necessity for Keynes to turn to confidence, or expectations about the future, as the final element in pulling his theory together; neither the internal logic of his Fundamental Equations nor the three elements of his new theory that were fresh at hand dictated that confidence should have been the next place for him to turn.[5] Only with reference to the external influence of business confidence can one see how the parts of *The General Theory* finally came together as a whole.

This is the story, then, that must be told in order to understand how Keynes built *The General Theory*. The model of expectations that he was to employ was unmistakably drawn from Frank Ramsey's subjective probabilities, but this application did not, or could not, take place until Keynes had embraced business confidence as a part of his theory.[6] Suddenly, two years after he had publicly abandoned his objective theory of probability and accepted Ramsey's criticisms, he had a place to use his own newly minted intersubjective probabilities. Thus, the process of intellectual discovery that led Keynes to *The General Theory* ended up being inextricably tied with the political sphere; only after he recognized the role that business confidence played in any program of recovery did Keynes see how to integrate the theoretical elements he was developing into a coherent whole.

Bringing Keynes to this point is a complicated matter, however, for he was the product of a tradition in economics that had relied for nearly 50 years on business confidence as an explanation of the trade cycle.[7] Robert

---

5. Michael Lawlor (1995) has carefully exhumed the record of Keynes's lectures on speculation and financial markets, from before the First World War. There is nothing, however, in his theoretical treatment of speculation in the currency markets or stock markets that necessitated its central role in macroeconomic theory. Lawlor argues, as against the thesis here, that uncertainty and expectations were already central to the *Treatise* and, thus, that there is no need to explain their introduction to *The General Theory*.

6. The important difference between Keynes's and Ramsey's use of subjective probabilities is that for Ramsey these probabilities were essentially individual, whereas for Keynes they were determined in large part by the group(s) to which one belonged. This important difference is explored most clearly by Donald Gillies and Grazia Ietto-Gillies 1991.

7. Skidelsky (1992) is apparently unaware of the Cambridge trade cycle tradition, or nineteenth-century monetary economics. Nothing else could account for the fictional dialogue he creates for Keynes before the Macmillan Committee (p. 323): "I am the first economist, I think to emphasize the speculative motive in investment decisions. . . ."

Skidelsky has completely overlooked this background to Keynes's thinking, for instance, and so posits that Keynes's interest in uncertainty in the
1920s was a new concern in economic theory. But to completely understand his conversion to confidence in 1933, one must first understand how
he escaped from this earlier tradition in Cambridge economics, for his
prior escape no doubt lent considerably to his refusal to entertain confidence seriously between 1930 and 1933. The story of how he rejected, and
then reembraced, confidence forms part of the affined mix of internal and
external elements that explain Keynes's nisus toward his *General Theory*.

With Her Magic Wand

At the time of his departure from the India Office in 1908 to return to
Cambridge as a lecturer in economics, Keynes was clearly a Marshallian
economist. In fact, his tutorials with Marshall prior to taking the civil
service examination constituted his only formal training in the subject.
But of course his father, Neville Keynes, was also a distinguished Cambridge economist and Maynard was quite literally raised in the tradition
of Cambridge economists. Thus from the time he returned to Cambridge
until the end of his life, he referred to the fact that he had been "brought
up" in the Cambridge tradition.[8]
    The influence of this upbringing was clear as early as 1911 in
Keynes's first serious work in monetary economics, his review of Irving
Fisher's *Purchasing Power of Money* in the *Economic Journal*. In the
review, Keynes is forced to begin by explaining that while books on
monetary economics were common in the States at this time because of
the policy controversies surrounding the dollar, they were nonexistent in
England.

> But this silence on the part of English economists, who have
> made no use of the advantage over their American colleagues which
> freedom from political controversy has given them, has greatly hin-
> dered the progress of the science, and the strange position has been
> reached that the theory of money, as it has been ordinarily under-
> stood and taught by academic economists in England for some time
> past, is considerably in advance of any published account of it. It is
> hardly an exaggeration to say that monetary theory, in its most

---

8. Moggridge (1976) summed up Keynes's early economics best in his chapter title,
"Glosses on Marshalliana: 1908–25." For an excellent recent treatment of Marshall's
monetary economics, see David Laidler 1991.

accurate form, has become in England a matter of oral tradition. These preliminary remarks are necessary in order to explain that it is from the standpoint of this oral tradition, rather than from that of any printed book, that an English economist must approach Professor Fisher's very important contribution to the subject.[9]

Keynes then goes on to explain that the outlines of this "oral tradition" can be found in Alfred Marshall's evidence before the Gold and Silver Commission in 1887 and before the Indian Currency Committee in 1898. With English monetary theory thus neatly collapsed to what Marshall said, Keynes goes on to use Marshall's explanation of how an increase in the stock of money is transmitted to the price level as a means of critiquing Fisher's book. But what matters in this story is not Keynes's glib self-assurance that what English economists say about the subject, when they happen to consider it at all, is better than what Americans can do in the course of a learned treatise; what matters is his explicit self-identification with Marshall's teachings on money.[10]

On one level, the level of pure theory, this self-identification would continue all the way through the *Treatise on Money*, where Keynes explained that he was merely working from Marshall's "real balance" version of the equation of exchange and attempting to make it more "dynamic" by the formal introduction of investment and saving to the model. On another level, however, Keynes had already begun his departure from the Cambridge orthodoxy. Marshall and Pigou both layered a verbal model of the trade cycle onto their real-balance version of the equation of exchange and it was at this nonanalytical level that Keynes first began to move away from his upbringing.

As is the case in many areas of economics, Marshall actually published very little on the trade cycle. And, true to form, what he did say he attempted to link with what had already been said by others.[11] Thus, his first discussion of the cycle in *The Economics of Industry* (1879) includes a long, approving quotation of "the famous words of Lord Overstone" to summarize his own position that the state of trade, "revolves apparently in an established cycle. First we find it in a state of quiescence,—next, improvement,—growing confidence,—prosperity,—excitement, overtrading,—convulsion,—pressure,—stagnation,—distress,—ending

---

9. Keynes 1911, 375–76.

10. Skidelsky's (1992) second volume of his biography of Keynes has a particularly good treatment of Keynes's anti-Americanism.

11. Because the passage quoted here comes from his book with his wife, Mary Paley Marshall, it is, of course, impossible to know exactly whose words we are reading.

again in quiescence."[12] In his own description of the cycle, Marshall begins with the ubiquitous "good harvest" of nineteenth-century economics and then proceeds to detail a series of events that arise from the fact that a good harvest drives food prices down and so leaves consumers with more disposable income to spend on manufactured goods. This leads to higher prices for these other commodities and this, in turn, leads to higher profits, greater output, an increased demand for labor, higher wages, yet greater demand for goods, and further rises in output. But behind all of this expansion lies confidence, for the rising tide of activity is facilitated by the confident expectations of lenders ("Credit is jubilant . . .") and leads to speculative activity on the part of overconfident producers who try to buy goods to sell them at a higher price. Eventually activity expands beyond the point at which all the goods being produced can be absorbed and lenders begin to become wary of making new loans and raise the interest rate on renewal loans; some speculators are forced to sell their goods to repay loans and this causes prices to stabilize or fall. At this point, everything reverses itself as prices and output fall in a spiral. "As credit by growing makes itself grow, so when distrust has taken the place of confidence, failure and panic breed panic and failure. The commercial storm leaves its path strewn with ruin. When it is over there is a calm, but a dull heavy calm."[13]

Marshall then considers the Malthusian idea of gluts, or insufficient consumer demand, as an alternative explanation of the repeated crises, but rejects it in favor of his own explanation of "commercial disorganization," or poor planning on the part of businessmen. "The chief cause of the evil is a want of confidence. The greater part of it could be removed almost in an instant if confidence could return, touch all industries with her magic wand, and make them continue their production and their demand for the wares of others."[14] Thus, in the most literal sense, confidence is an exogenous factor in Marshall's theory, floating in and out to make things happen, neither a reflection of real conditions nor an integral part (that is to say, an endogenous part) of the theory. Marshall actually repeats a large part of this argument verbatim in his *Principles* (1890) and elaborates on it in *Money, Credit and Commerce* (1923, 261) only to the extent of suggesting that greater collection and dissemination of economic information could bolster confidence and help alleviate some of the waves of overconfidence and distrust.

---

12. Marshall and Marshall 1879, 153.
13. Ibid., 153.
14. Ibid., 154–55.

As in so many other areas, Pigou played Aristotle to Marshall's Plato in the theory of the trade cycle; Pigou's main achievement was to classify and codify every possible permutation of his mentor's teachings. Thus, in the long series of books that he wrote on macroeconomic topics, he continued to refine and elaborate the way that confidence affected the trade cycle. The pinnacle of this exercise was his breaking out section 6 of his *Economics of Welfare* (1920), which dealt with the trade cycle, and making it into a separate book, *Industrial Fluctuations* (1927). But although Pigou makes a clear and sensible distinction between real causes, psychological causes, and autonomous monetary causes of the cycle, and considers each at some length, his conclusion is that the psychological forces are impossible to separate out from the other causes. "Thus, while recognizing that the varying expectations of businessmen may themselves be in part a psychological reflex of such things as good and bad harvests . . . we conclude definitely that they (expectations), and not anything else, constitute the immediate and direct causes or antecedents of industrial fluctuations" (1927, 33–34). Pigou's most enduring legacy in cycle theory may have been his coining of the phrase "errors of optimism and pessimism" to describe the cycles of confidence and distrust that he borrowed from Marshall.[15]

In retrospect, one of the most remarkable things about Marshall's and Pigou's position on the trade cycle is that it represented such an inconsistency in their analytical frameworks.[16] Both men, in their strictly microeconomic arguments, insisted that expectations of the future were objective matters that could be handled formally in the same manner as any other variable. Uncertainty is "an *objective* property which all well informed persons would estimate in the same way."[17] The idea that uncertainty or expectations present an essentially subjective element involving a regular pattern of error simply does not follow from what either theorist said in the microeconomic sections of his work.

The response to this type of ad hoc explanation of the trade cycle was varied among the generation of Cambridge economists who followed Pigou. It might seem natural in retrospect that the younger economists would seize on the inconsistency in their predecessors' thought to forge new theoretical advances, but this was not the case. Those, like Dennis Robertson and Frederick Lavington, who were largely Mar-

---

15. But see the essay by David Collard (1983) that makes Pigou the predecessor of the modern new classical-cum-rational expectationist school of thought.

16. See Robert J. Bigg 1990 on this subject.

17. This quotation comes from the eighth edition of Marshall's *Principles* (1923, 77, italics in the original).

shallian, made efforts to more clearly articulate the real and monetary factors in the cycle without altering Marshall's basic insight regarding the importance of confidence. Others, like Ralph Hawtrey, who had not studied economics while at Cambridge and had come to the subject only in his work at the Treasury, eschewed confidence altogether to focus on the effects of interest rates on traders' stocks (i.e., their inventories). Keynes, who as late as 1923 still happily identified himself with the Marshallian approach to monetary theory proper, followed an unpredictable and uneven path in severing himself from the Cambridge trade cycle tradition. In 1910, he appears to have been very orthodox. In an essay entitled "Great Britain's Foreign Investments" in the *Political Quarterly* (1910), he addressed the entrepreneur's motivations for investing and could not have sounded more Marshallian.

> Moreover, he will be affected, as is obvious, not by the net income which he will actually receive from his investment in the long run, but by his expectations. These will often depend upon fashion, upon advertisement, or upon irrational waves of optimism or depression.[18]

Nineteen years later, however, in the drafting of the *Treatise,* he had apparently become a skeptic.

> When it is said that the credit cycle is a monetary phenomenon, it is not meant that the initiating causes of the disturbance are necessarily or usually of a monetary character. If the increase in the demand for credit, or the decrease in the supply of it, is due in the first instance to nothing but an actual or prospective inflation, then indeed the initiating cause is itself monetary. If the increase in the demand for credit is a reaction from a previous slump which was itself the final phase of a previous credit cycle, then the initiating cause is monetary in the sense that it arose out of a previous failure to remedy a defect in the monetary machinery. But even when the initiating cause is of an entirely nonmonetary character, such as wars, the variability of harvests, the progress of invention, or even *Professor Pigou's somewhat mythical "psychological errors of optimism and pessimism" on the part of the business world,* it is only through the reaction of these events on the monetary machine that the credit cycle can develop.[19]

---

18. Keynes 1910, 39.
19. This draft fragment is reproduced in *JMK*, xiii, 89, italics added.

This passage did not survive to the *Treatise* itself, but a much more humorous expression of his skepticism regarding confidence occurs there when he explains how a misunderstanding of the real nature of the cycle can lead to an interpretation in terms of Pigou's "errors."

> For example, a changeover in the type of production from investment goods to consumption goods (or *vice versa*) does not, on account of the period occupied by the process of production, produce its results in the market until after an appreciable time has elapsed. Thus, as we have seen, the price stimulus to a changeover is apt to be continued until some time after the necessary steps have been taken. The result often is that the remedy is overdone. It is as though the family were to go on giving a child successive doses of castor oil every ten minutes until the first dose had done its work. Or—to take a better parallel—it is as though different members of the family were to give successive doses to the child, each in ignorance of the doses given by the others. The child will be very ill. Bismuth will then be administered on the same principle. Scientists will announce that children are subject to a diarrhoea—constipation cycle, due, they will add, to the weather, or, failing that, to alternations of optimism and pessimism amongst the members of the family.[20]

The clear implication is that confidence is an erroneous explanation offered by people who do not understand the underlying real causes of a disturbance.

In the intervening twenty years, Keynes had never stopped writing about expectations and confidence, but the emphasis they received and the importance that he attributed to them had changed radically.[21]

Intelligent Anticipation

Only three years after his essay in the *Political Quarterly* that spoke of "irrational waves of optimism or depression," and marked him as a Marshallian trade cycle adherent, Keynes was to offer a theory of the

---

20. Keynes 1930, vol. 2, 223.
21. An important difference between my interpretation and Lawlor's (1995) is that Lawlor takes Keynes's comments on speculation and uncertainty in 1930 to play a central role in his economics, while I argue that they are not integrated into his central message.

cycle almost completely devoid of confidence. In a paper delivered to the Political Economy Club in London in December 1913, Keynes laid out an explanation for the trade cycle along quite different lines. The paper, entitled "How far are Bankers Responsible for the Alternations of Crisis and Depression?" draws from work that Dennis Robertson was doing at the time, and attempts to explain how the cycle is a result of alternations between overlending and underlending on the part of bankers.[22] As was true throughout his career, Keynes develops his theory around a set of novel definitions that make it difficult for a first-time reader to easily penetrate the argument. But the gist of the paper is simple enough: when banks lend out more for capital investment than has been deposited in savings (i.e., they also lend out a part of their transactions deposits), this leads first to expansion and then to a downturn as the "overlending" results (necessarily) in default because of the insufficient funds available to support the increased investment. This, in turn, causes saving to be greater than investment. Keynes does not discuss the process by which underlending leads to an upturn, but presumably the economy moves back into a state of overlending for the same reason(s) that it initially occurred.

The initial reason(s) for an upturn are interesting to note, for while Keynes suggests at one point that "feelings of confidence and enterprise"[23] may spur the initial demand for bank loans that leads to the overlending, he later qualifies this by noting that past demand for loans has not arisen from "rash or overoptimistic development in directions which are not *really* profitable or desirable in the long run."[24] The problem, rather, is that there exists a surfeit of profitable opportunities and too easy a facility for underwriting new projects that do not have legitimate financial backing. Thus, expectations of future yield and confidence are perfectly reasonable; there are just not enough savings to go around.

Following the war and the severe round of inflation and deflation in 1919–21, however, Keynes adopted yet another explanation of the cycle. This new explanation relied heavily on expectations, but in a new and different way. As his ideas developed in this period, he increasingly moved to an explanation of the cycle that depended on businessmen's *correct expectation* that the authorities would allow prices to rise and fall. A key step in his movement to this theory of "intelligent anticipa-

22. This paper is reprinted in *JMK,* xiii, 2–14.
23. Ibid., 8.
24. Ibid., 11, italics added.

tions" was his explanation of recent events as depending upon a one-time massive error in business expectations brought about by unpredictable changes in government fiscal policy.

In the first of his pieces discussing this episode, a September 1921 *Sunday Times* article, "The Depression of Trade" (1921b), Keynes relies heavily on "the exceptional range of miscalculation" of businessmen as the explanation for the boom and bust. Businessmen are said to have speculated in inventories because of the rapid postwar inflations and thereby to have exacerbated the inflation. Eventually, however, prices rose above the level at which consumers could pay and massive liquidations followed as the inventories were sold off. This not only forced prices down, but curtailed employment as prices fell below costs of production and manufacturers ceased operation. But Keynes makes clear that these miscalculations on the part of the businessmen were not a part of a *recurring* pattern of forecasting errors.

> The causes of such fluctuations are various and disputed. Like its predecessors, the recent depression has been of complex origin. But a bad season in Asia and the miscalculations of merchants have played the biggest part. No doubt the war has been indirectly responsible, because the severity of the crisis has been due to the exceptional range of miscalculation, which the terrific fluctuations in prices consequent on the budgetary policies of governments have brought about, and also by the inapplicability of prewar standards as a guide to what was normal. These helped business to lose its bearings and to drift far out of its course.[25]

In today's infelicitous jargon, one would say that the businessmen forecast badly in this particular case because of a "structural break" in the economy; what were reasonable assumptions before the war became miscalculations in the changed postwar world.

By the next year, when his articles on European Reconstruction appeared in the *Manchester Guardian Commercial* (1922), Keynes was much less interested in the moment of the structural break than he was in the normally accurate expectations that businessmen employed in following the rise in prices. The fourth of these articles, which became chapter 1 of *A Tract on Monetary Reform* in 1923, deals with the effects of inflation and deflation on the economy and details how wide swings in the price level affect savings, investment, and wages. In the context of

---

25. Keynes 1921b.

this discussion he once again talks about how businessmen speculated on inventory during the inflation of 1919–20, but now he does not dwell on the errors in their forecasts of continued price increases. In fact, he never uses the word *error* to describe business expectations in the *Tract*. Instead he begins calling them "intelligent anticipations."

Take, for example, the *Statist* index number for raw materials month by month from April 1919 to March 1920:

April 1919	100	October	127
May	108	November	131
June	112	December	135
July	117	January 1920	142
August	120	February	150
September	121	March	146

It follows from this table that a man, who borrowed money from his banker and used the proceeds to purchase raw materials selected at random, stood to make a profit in every single month of this period with the exception of the last, and would have cleared 46 percent on the average of the year. Yet bankers were not charging at this time above 7 percent for their advances, leaving a clear profit of between 30 and 40 percent per annum, without the exercise of any particular skill, to any person lucky enough to have embarked on these courses. How much more were the opportunities of persons whose business position and expert knowledge enabled them to exercise intelligent anticipation as to the probable course of prices of particular commodities! Yet any dealer in or user of raw materials on a large scale who knew his trade was thus situated.[26]

Although he does not discuss the reason for this shift to "intelligent expectations," the answer may be found in chapter 2 of the *Tract* where he describes in great detail the course of the hyperinflations in Germany, Austria, and Russia. In his vivid accounts of the distorted behavior that sprang from these social crises, Keynes makes it clear that people adapt very quickly to such price changes; this recognition may have helped move him away from the idea that pervasive errors lay behind the boom and the slump.

Perhaps the strongest statement of Keynes's sense of the accuracy

---

26. Keynes 1923a, 18.

and importance of business expectations at this time can be found in his defense of an activist approach to price stabilization. He first argues that the swings in employment and output that characterize the cycle are based on a reasonable expectation that the price level will fluctuate, and this leads to his argument that the cure for the cycle is to establish a reasonable expectation of price stability.

It is one of the objects of this book to urge that the best way to cure this mortal disease of individualism is to provide that there shall never exist any confident expectation either that prices generally are going to fall or that they are going to rise; and also that there shall be no serious risk that a movement, if it does occur, will be a big one. If, unexpectedly and accidentally, a moderate movement were to occur, wealth, though it might be redistributed, would not be diminished thereby.

To procure this result by removing all possible influences towards an initial movement, whether such influences are to be found in the skies only or everywhere, would seem to be a hopeless enterprise. The remedy would lie, rather, in so controlling the standard of value that, whenever something occurred which, left to itself, would create an expectation of a change in the general level of prices, the controlling authority should take steps to counteract this expectation by setting in motion some factor of a contrary tendency. Even if such a policy were not wholly successful, either in counteracting expectations or in avoiding actual movements, it would be an improvement on the policy of sitting quietly by, whilst a standard of value, governed by chance causes and deliberately removed from central control, produces expectations which paralyse or intoxicate the government of production.[27]

Such an account of businessmen riding the recent changes in prices up and down with reasonable accuracy does not account for the turning points in the cycle, of course, but in an interesting aside later in chapter 5, Keynes notes that "it is beyond the scope of this volume to deal adequately with the diagnosis and analysis of the credit cycle."[28] This observation would appear to lend credence to the argument that Keynes is not after a Marshallian explanation of the cycle in chapter 1 of the *Tract,* for although he has gone much further than Marshall in elaborat-

---

27. Keynes 1923a, 35.
28. Keynes 1923a, 148.

ing how businessmen's expectations can cause changes in output and employment, he is explicitly arguing that this explanation should *not* be taken as a theory of the cycle. Instead, he seems to be arguing that expectations are an accurate reflection of real events, something that *tracks* the cycle rather than something that causes it.

The idea that expectations and confidence are important to the cycle, but not as errors that cause the cycle, is also manifest in a speech that Keynes gave to the Liberal Summer School as the *Tract* was in press. The speech, which also appeared the following week in *The Nation* as "Currency Policy and Unemployment" (1923b) explains "that a *general expectation* of falling prices may inhibit the productive process altogether."[29] The question of errors in judgment or waves of irrationality never enters Keynes's picture; all that matters to his story is that widespread unemployment will result from the business world's quite reasonable expectation that the stated policy of deflation will be carried out.

A deliberate policy of deflation, however, greatly aggravates the situation. In so far as the business world believe that those responsible for currency policy really intend to carry out a declared policy of deflation, they are bound to feel some lack of confidence in the existing price level, in which case they will naturally draw in their horns to a certain extent with the result of diminishing employment. For this reason a modern industrial community organized on lines of individualistic capitalism simply cannot stand a declared policy of deflation. The business world, it is true, can save its pocket to a certain extent by refraining from new enterprises for the time being. But it can only do this at the expense of passing on to the rest of the community a heavy burden of unemployment and of unemployment doles.[30]

In any event, it seems difficult to describe this explanation of the Slump as Marshallian; the expectations in question are neither erroneous nor exogenous to the system.

Calculating on a Probability

If Keynes was an adherent of some type of theory of "intelligent anticipations" in the *Tract*, this position would have been perfectly

---

29. Keynes 1923b.
30. Ibid.

consistent with what he had said two years earlier in *Probability*. Having dropped his rhetoric of irrationality as regards businessmen's expectations, he now seemed to have a corps of quite reasonable individuals who went about intuiting the logical relations that connected propositions about the future with their knowledge of the facts.

This is explicit in the original (1922) version of "The Consequences to Society of Changes in the Value of Money" that appeared in the *Manchester Guardian Commercial* and in its revised form (1923a) as chapter 1 of the *Tract*. In the course of discussing businessmen's decisions to borrow in order to finance new investment, Keynes addresses the question of the effect of changes in the real rate of interest brought about by fluctuations in the price level. In the earlier version in the *Manchester Guardian Commercial* he explicitly refers to borrowers "calculating on a probability."[31]

> It is true that in a period of rapidly changing prices it is impossible for the money rate of interest, which is affected by other influences also, to adjust itself adequately or fast enough to prevent the real rate of interest from becoming abnormal. But even in such times a rise or fall (as the case may be) in the money rate of interest may nevertheless exercise a decisive influence on speculative movements, inasmuch as the merchant, who borrows money to take advantage of a prospective low real rate of interest, has to act in advance of the rise in prices and is calculating on a probability, not upon a certainty, with the result that he will be deterred by a movement in the money rate of interest of much less magnitude than the contrary movement in the real rate of interest, upon which indeed he is reckoning, yet is not reckoning with certainty.[32]

Now, of course, one could argue that this reference to calculation is only meant metaphorically, but this interpretation would seem impossible to reconcile with his revision of the passage a year later for the *Tract*.

> Nevertheless in a period of rapidly changing prices, the money rate of interest seldom adjusts itself adequately or fast enough to prevent the real rate from becoming abnormal. For it is not the *fact* of a given rise of prices, but the *expectation* of a rise compounded of

---

31. Keynes 1922, 327.
32. Ibid.

the various possible price movements and the estimated probability of each, which affects money rates; and in countries where the currency has not collapsed completely, there has seldom or never existed a sufficient general confidence in a further rise or fall of prices to cause the short-money rate of interest to rise above 10 percent per annum, or to fall below 1 percent.[33]

The only problem with taking this passage as a direct statement of Keynes's position in *Probability* would seem to be his strong position there against an assumption that probabilities are numerical. Are these businessmen and their mathematical expectation of the future price level ("the *expectation* of a rise compounded of the various possible price movements and the estimated probability of each") too calculating to be agents from *Probability?*

This would not seem to be the case if one considers Keynes's full argument in *Probability.*[34] In his discussion of the measurability of probability, Keynes considers the question of whether organized insurance markets indicate the inherent measurability of probabilities and comes to a mixed conclusion: "In fact underwriters themselves distinguish between risks which are properly insurable, either because their probability can be estimated between comparatively narrow numerical limits or because it is possible to make a 'book' which covers all possibilities, and other risks which cannot be dealt with in this way. . . ."[35] Keynes refers to this first class of probabilities again later when he says, "if we can place a probability in an order of magnitude with some standard probability, we can obtain its approximate measure by comparison."[36] It seems reasonable to assume that these are the "estimated" probabilities to which he refers in the revision of his article for the *Tract.*

If businessmen employ these numerically approximate probabilities in forming their expectations of changes in the price level, then the duty of the monetary authorities, in Keynes's eyes, is to damp the fluctuations so that the mean price change is lowered. The reduction in such intelligent anticipations of the price level will, as a result, reduce

---

33. Keynes 1923a, 20, italics in the original.

34. Although Brady 1993 may be faulted for his treatment of Keynes's formula for risk, he must receive credit for being one of the few to emphasize Keynes's practical concern with the measurement of probabilities.

35. Keynes 1921a, 23–24.

36. Ibid., 160.

fluctuations in investment, output, and employment.[37] The rational agents of *A Treatise on Probability* can be induced to stabilize the economy through their intelligent anticipations of a more rational monetary policy.

The Magic Formula Mentality

The distance that Keynes had traveled from Marshall by 1923 can easily be seen in his use of the word *confidence*. Rather than a disembodied concept involving the mood of the business world ("confidence with her magic wand . . ."), Keynes characterized confidence as a matter of a calculated expectation about the future price level. He speaks repeatedly in the *Tract* and in his address to the Liberal Summer School (1921b) about "the lack of confidence" as the cause of a slump, but this is always qualified as "the lack of confidence *in the existing level of prices.*" In the context of his statements about readily calculable "intelligent" expectations, this lack of confidence refers to a *determinate expectation* about the difference between the current and the future price level; the expectation set up by the change in government policy.

But if we are not surprised that the author of *A Treatise on Probability* should travel such a distance from his economics tutor, neither should we be surprised that his use of expectations and confidence had changed considerably by the time of the publication of *A Treatise on Money* in 1930. In the interim, we know that Keynes had extensive contact with Frank Ramsey in Cambridge and that he had already acknowledged considerable doubt about his own position on probability by 1926; by 1930, when he wrote his eloquent obituary for Ramsey, he was quite likely even further along in his own self-doubt. This would seem to be the evidence, in any case, from the *Treatise,* where expectations play a very uneven role and appear sometimes quite reasonable and at other times quite unreasonable.[38]

Clearly, however, his beliefs regarding the nature of probability were not central to the construction of the *Treatise.* Already driven by a personal ambition to write the definitive work on monetary theory,

---

37. Meltzer (1988) has captured this aspect of Keynes's early monetary policy concerns better than anyone else.

38. As Meltzer (1988, 56) says of Keynes's use of expectations in the *Treatise,* "Anticipations, or expectations, are a deus ex machina that enter or leave at convenient places." Moggridge (1976, 96) notes that "Rather than arising in asides, as in the *Treatise,* uncertainty dominated the *General Theory.*"

Keynes's concerns with policy soon emerged as a parallel force driving him to find an instrument that he could use to influence government decision making. This desire to have a powerful analytical tool to influence policymakers undoubtedly exacerbated his tendency to employ a magic formula mentality in his theoretical work and it was the predominance of this mentality that was most responsible for the minor role of expectations in the *Treatise*.

The centerpiece of the *Treatise* is Keynes's Fundamental Equations. These two adaptations of the equation of exchange are pieces of classical monetary theory in their focus on the price level; they are meant quite literally to elucidate the forces that cause the price level to change. But although Keynes's adaptation is original and clever, it runs into all the problems of classical monetary theory and the equation of exchange: it is tautological, it assumes full employment, and it is devoid of any behavioral implications (without the addition of numerous ad hoc assumptions). But like generations before (and after) him, Keynes was enamored of the simple power of the model. To be sure, he was critical of many of the traditional assumptions used in trying to force causal relations out of the model, and had been since the *Tract,* but he still fell victim to the facile power of the equation's tautological tightness. That is, when faced with several simple aggregates that must by definition go up (or down) in unison, he resorted to improvised and ad hoc explanations of the behaviors that caused these related movements. Nothing in the equation itself dictates any behavior in relation to the movements of the aggregates. The apparent freedom created by this lack of behavioral dictates easily leads to incompatible or inconsistent stories to explain the movements. Thus it is that expectations come to serve largely as a deus ex machina in the *Treatise;* they are a device that enters and leaves Keynes's story at convenient points to solve problems, but they form no necessary part of his story and are never made a complete part of the whole.[39]

There is, of course, a nice irony in this ad hoc use of expectations. The *Treatise* is a book meant to explain the trade cycle (defined in the classical sense of fluctuations in prices) and to do so in a way that departs significantly from Pigou's "mythical" errors of optimism and pessimism; and yet, in the end, Keynes is left employing expectations in an ad hoc way just as Marshall and Pigou had. The difference is that Marshall and Pigou used expectations as the crux of their theory of the cycle, whereas for Keynes they are *ancillary* to the theory of the cycle

---

39. See the previous note.

implied in his Fundamental Equations. Nonetheless, Keynes ends up employing ad hocery no less than Marshall and Pigou.

This ad hocery can be seen clearly in Keynes's discussion of the demand for savings deposits. Because this concept looks like a nascent version of *The General Theory's* liquidity preference function, it is often taken as the key place to look for expectations in the *Treatise.* Its role within the overall theoretical framework could not be more different, however.[40] Liquidity preference in *The General Theory* plays a co-equal role as one of several functions that are necessary to determine the economy's position; the demand for savings deposits in the *Treatise,* on the other hand, is only a part of a background explanation of how the prices of investment goods change in the course of the trade cycle.

In fact, Keynes's discussion of changes in the prices of investment goods is *itself* an ad hoc construction in the context of his Fundamental Equations. The purpose of the *Treatise* and the Fundamental Equations is to explain changes in the *general* price level, which Keynes subdivides into the prices of *consumption* goods and *investment* goods; when the algebra is done, however, Keynes ends up with equations for the general price level and for consumption goods, but with no equation for the price of investment goods. Thus, he attempts an explanation of this other part of his theory only in verbal terms, outside the analytical apparatus he has so carefully crafted.

In this verbal explanation of changes in the price level of investment goods, bank deposits play a crucial role for two reasons, both of which depend on what seems today to be the awkward implicit assumption that the market value of a firm's stock is equal to the net book value of its assets. This assumption makes movements in a firm's stock price equivalent to changes in the price of investment goods, which, in turn, makes savings deposits important both because they represent an alternative asset to stocks and because they are a potential source of funds for banks to invest in the stock market. Uncertainty and expectations enter the argument largely by way of the first of these. An individual chooses to hold savings deposits in his portfolio, in part, on the basis of his expectation of the future price of stocks: if stock prices are expected to rise, he holds more stock and less savings deposits; if stock prices are expected to fall, he holds more savings deposits.

This ad hoc argument within an ad hoc argument provides a pregnant analytical suggestion, but it remains one that is undeveloped for the sim-

---

40. Patinkin (1976, 40, 81) emphasizes the difference between the treatment of the demand for savings in the *Treatise* and of liquidity preference in *The General Theory.*

ple reason that it is only being used to fill in the background to the real engine of his analysis, the Fundamental Equations. The demand for savings deposits could only become a part of the more fully conceived liquidity preference function after Keynes had dropped the Fundamental Equations, fully embraced a subjective theory of probability, and returned to an explanation of the trade cycle in terms of business confidence.[41]

Two other undeveloped, ad hoc treatments of uncertainty appear in the *Treatise* in Keynes's discussions of investment demand and the term structure of interest rates. The two come together in a nicely connected way in Keynes's climactic chapter 37 on "The Control of the Rate of Investment." Here Keynes reaches the logical conclusion of his two volumes and asks, "But when all is said and done, does it lie within the power of a central bank in actual practice to pursue a policy which will have the effect of fixing the value of money at any prescribed level?"[42] The crux of the problem for Keynes lies in finding a reasonable way to connect the central bank's chief tool, bank rate, to long-term investment. Since bank rate is a short-term rate of interest, there is no obvious reason to expect that it would affect the rate of investment on fixed capital. Keynes very resourcefully employs an expectational argument, however, in regards to both investment demand and the term structure to obtain his desideratum. But as in the case of the demand for savings deposits, they are improvised arguments ancillary to the main framework.

Keynes's concern with the term structure of interest rates is perhaps somewhat of a surprise to the contemporary economist who was raised on the post-*General Theory* literature in macroeconomics. One of the canards in that literature is that Keynes had no theory of the term structure and that the recognition of his oversight led others to pathbreaking theoretical work in macroeconomics and finance. But while it is true that an impressive analytical artifice was constructed on the back of this straw man, it is also the case that Keynes was very concerned with the term structure and this concern played a key role

---

41. Skidelsky's (1992, 444) explicit attempt to create a story in which uncertainty is the continuous strand in Keynes's economic thought seems to lead him away from seeing the necessity of explaining the many steps in this process. Thus, in addition to ignoring the Cambridge trade cycle tradition, he argues throughout his book as if each of Keynes's statements, regardless of date or emphasis, is a part of an unchanging theoretical concern. Patinkin (1976, 141; 1982, 6; 1990, 219) seems to make a similar error in arguing that since Keynes's treatment of uncertainty was equivalent to Frank Knight's in his classic *Risk, Uncertainty, and Profit* (1921), there is no novelty, or story, to Keynes's concern with these issues. Patinkin is incorrect both to equate Keynes's concern with Knight's and to imply that Keynes had one unchanging concern with probability and expectations.

42. Keynes 1930, vol. 2, 304.

in his striving toward *The General Theory*. From the time he took up the question of how to reconcile the control of bank rate with the control of fixed investment, his concern with the term structure never diminished.[43]

In the *Treatise*, Keynes offers two arguments for supposing that changes in bank rate will cause changes in long-term rates of interest (and hence investment). While both of these are, of necessity, "tacked onto" his underlying analysis of the Fundamental Equations, they at least have the benefit of being based on extensive data. In retrospect, they also both seem quite prescient, as they suggest eventual developments in portfolio choice theory.[44]

The first of his arguments for a connection between short- and long-run rates of interest is really a direct application of the later insights of portfolio choice theory. Keynes argues that if short-term rates fall below long-term rates, then this will cause investors to sell their short-term securities and buy longer-dated instruments in order to take advantage of the rate differential. This will, of course, cause the price of long bonds to be bid up, and their effective yield will fall. Keynes helps the process along, however, by suggesting that investors will expect these rises in the price of long-term bonds (i.e., they will become bullish on long bonds when the price of short bonds rises); thus, they are motivated to buy the long bonds both by the rate differential and by their expectations.

Keynes's second argument only tangentially involves expectations, though, had he been more systematic, he might have made the same case regarding expectations that he had made in his first argument regarding the connection between changes in long and short rates. This second argument involves banks and other financial institutions (e.g., insurance companies) and concerns their need to maintain a minimum level of income to avoid injury to their reputations. In this case, when short rates fall sufficiently, the institutions are compelled to shift to longer-dated securities and the same run up in prices and drop in yields results as in the previous case. Keynes refers to the possibility that institutions may have a "serious reason . . . for positively fearing long-term securities at their existing price level," which presumably is a reference to anticipations of rising rather than falling long rates, but he goes no further than this in explicitly discussing expectations in his second argument.

Keynes concludes his discussion of the term structure, however, on a very odd note, with an argument that is completely concerned with

---

43. See especially Moggridge and Howson 1974.
44. Lawlor (1995) explains the portfolio choice nature of Keynes's work very well.

expectations but that does not directly involve the term structure at all. This represents yet another ad hoc treatment of expectations.

At the end of his discussion of the term structure, he undertakes a three-page digression on the stock market as an example of how expectations based purely on short-run phenomena can influence long-run variables. And, although his argument revolves solely around how equity prices fluctuate on short-term news, the argument by extension is that long-run bond prices suffer the same fluctuations.

But while one might suppose that this argument about the stock market is remarkable because it foreshadows much of what Keynes says in *The General Theory* about investment, the more remarkable thing about the argument is the inconsistency it reveals in the *Treatise*. To see just how far Keynes could travel from his theoretical structure when he engaged in an ad hoc argument, one need only compare his statements in chapter 37 about the stock market with his treatment ten chapters earlier in chapter 27, "Fluctuations in the Rate of Investment." There, in his formal treatment, he never mentions the type of argument that appears in his discussion of the term structure of interest rates. What one gets in the earlier chapter is a theory of investment in which changes in expectations of future profits depend solely on inventions and new technologies; that is, expectations are presented as an accurate reflection of changing real conditions. The earlier chapter is totally devoid of the type of confidence argument that Pigou advocated in *Industrial Fluctuations*. The fact of his distance from Pigou in this regard is perhaps best illustrated by noting that Keynes explicitly embraces Joseph Schumpeter's theory of investment in the *Treatise,* whereas this is the type of theory (devoid of confidence) that Pigou dismisses.[45] Keynes's ad hoc use of expectations could not be more clear; expectations might be useful as a part of a digression to make a point, but they formed no part of his central argument.

But before leaving Keynes's treatment of expectations in this context, there is a second feature of Keynes's discussion of the stock market that is noteworthy, for not only has the *economic* nature of his argument changed since the *Tract;* the *philosophical* nature of his argument has changed, too.

---

45. The extent of Keynes's distaste for Pigou's *Industrial Fluctuations* is also evident in a letter from Ralph Hawtrey on 7 October 1928. "I am glad to find you take the same sort of view as I do of Pigou's book . . . there is so very much to disagree with and so little to accept." This letter is reprinted in *JMK,* xiii, 76–77.

How far the motives which I have been attributing above to the market are strictly rational, I leave it to others to judge. They are best regarded, I think, as an example of how sensitive—over-sensitive if you like—to the near future, about which we may think that we know a little, even the best-informed must be, because, in truth, we know almost nothing about the more remote future. And the exaggerations of this same tendency, to which we now come, also play a part.[46]

Keynes demurs from answering his question about rationality, "I leave it to others to judge," and goes on, in the vein of Ramsey, to say, "For part of the explanation which we are seeking is to be found in psychological phenomenon which appears even more strikingly in the current market valuation of ordinary shares." Not only has Keynes abandoned his idea from the *Tract* that businessmen anticipate the future intelligently, he also appears in this aside to have abandoned his earlier conception of probability. Whereas he had said in *Probability* that probability is objective and explicitly denied its subjective character, now he is willing to characterize expectations of the future as psychological. Keynes may still not have gone the whole distance to Ramsey's position at this point, but what he says is so strikingly like his comments in his review of the *Foundations of Mathematics* that it is difficult to discern any significant difference.[47]

Confidence Lost

Despite Keynes's use of expectations and uncertainty in the *Treatise,* it is reasonably clear that these play no central role in either his analytical apparatus or the vision that underlies it. The most obvious manifestation of this in his work of the period is his steadfast refusal to accept contemporaneous explanations of the Slump that relied on speculation in the New York stock market for their fulcrum.[48] Expectations were occasionally handy as a way of talking out what was going on behind the scenes, but their treatment was so ad hoc that when Keynes went off on an "expectational tangent," it apparently did not even occur to him that his

---

46. Keynes 1930, vol. 2, 322.
47. Lawlor (1995) uses this same quotation to argue that Keynes's positions on uncertainty and expectations are the same in the *Treatise* and *The General Theory.*
48. See Keynes's writings in 1928 (*JMK,* xiii, 52–77) and his treatment of this topic two years later in the *Treatise* (*JMK,* vi, 170–77). Keynes initially refused to recognize the importance of speculation to price changes, though he later gave it a "secondary" role.

argument might contradict what was said elsewhere in the book. But perhaps this theoretical inconsistency is what he meant when he said that the book was an "artistic failure." At any rate, if Keynes believed that expectations were crucial to his story in the *Treatise,* he never found a way to say this explicitly. They remain a deus ex machina.

Thus, through a process with at least two steps, Keynes had placed himself firmly outside the Cambridge confidence tradition by 1930. First, in the *Tract,* he developed an idea of intelligent expectations. Then in the *Treatise,* he developed a theory of the trade cycle that provided no central role for expectations. Instead, Keynes offered a theory of how a disequilibrium between the market and the natural rate of interest caused a disequilibrium between savings and investment and how it was the mechanical repetition of these disequilibria that accounted for the business cycle. With the advent of a "scientific theory of booms and slumps" it would no longer be necessary to misdiagnose the bismuth-castor oil cycle as resulting from errors of optimism and pessimism. Keynes was enough of a believer in his magic formula to relegate Marshall's and Pigou's theory of the trade cycle to the realm of the "mythical."

But his liberation from the "mythical" errors of optimism and pessimism was soon relegated to the dustbin of history by Keynes himself. After the publication of *The General Theory,* when he repeatedly complained that orthodox economics was "concerned with a simplified world where there is always full employment, and where doubt and fluctuations of confidence are ruled out," he was more nearly describing his own position in the *Treatise* than he was the work of Marshall or Pigou. For while Marshall and Pigou were guilty of an inconsistency between their micro-and macroeconomic arguments, they did take "doubt and fluctuations of confidence" to be an important part of their story. It had been Keynes, not his mentors, who had tried to minimize the role of confidence and expectations in monetary theory.

Keynes could legitimately claim that he was the first theorist to put together an analytical model that could incorporate expectations and confidence in an integral way, but in his purposefully inflated rhetoric he claimed not that he had solved an inconsistency in Cambridge monetary theory, but that he was the first to even *see the need* to consider confidence.[49] But while his old friend Dennis Robertson complained to him

---

49. Skidelsky (1992) is one in a long line of interpreters to be taken in by Keynes's story. See above, note 7.

of his unfair treatment of Marshall and Pigou, Keynes persisted in his rhetoric in the hope of jarring people and getting them to pay attention to his book.

Once again, however, the horse is set before the cart. So far we have only seen how Keynes purged confidence from monetary theory. What remains to be seen is how confidence re-entered his arguments after 1930 and moved back to center stage.

CHAPTER 5

Confidence Regained

The most surprising part of the story so far is undoubtedly the fact of Keynes's clear departure from the Cambridge confidence tradition in the *Treatise*. Although no one talked seriously (if at all) about the role of confidence in *The General Theory* at its 25th anniversary in 1961, it is now a commonplace that the book's central message is concerned with long-term expectations and the state of business confidence. Following the pathbreaking historical work of G. L. S. Shackle in the 1960s, the post-Keynesians have turned this commonplace into a cottage industry and now economists of virtually every stripe acknowledge the place of confidence in *The General Theory*.[1]

But where did this concern come from?[2] Many people have pointed to Keynes's concern with bulls and bears in his treatment of the demand for savings deposits in the *Treatise,* but as we have seen, this is an undeveloped part of the book. More to the point is the fact that his trajectory to the *Treatise* actually involved a move *away* from confidence and expectations. Keynes's concern with bulls and bears in the *Treatise* is undeveloped and ad hoc because he was explicitly uninterested in confidence arguments. In an effort to provide a "scientific explanation" of the trade cycle, Keynes became so engrossed in his magic formula mentality that he abandoned his Cambridge heritage in business confidence.

Thus, the question is not how Keynes saw his way to develop his unsystematic observations in the *Treatise* into his theoretical centerpiece;

---

1. Patinkin (1990, 215–16) dates the beginning of the focus on uncertainty in Keynes's writings from 1961. He chooses that year because of the publication of G. L. S. Shackle's survey article, "Recent Theories Concerning the Nature and Role of Interest," which can arguably be identified as the font of the literature concerned with uncertainty in Keynes's writing.

2. Moggridge (1986, 362) was the first to explicitly point out that no one writing on Keynes's concern with uncertainty has been able to adequately explain why the concern was not manifest before *The General Theory*. Why, he asks, would Keynes's interest not have surfaced in the *Tract* (1923a) or the *Treatise* (1930), if it was merely a manifestation of his concerns in *Probability* (1921a)?

it is how he came to overcome his deep-seated animus toward confidence and make it pivotal in *The General Theory*.[3] The answer lies in his work in policy making. From early 1930, when he was working on the final draft of the *Treatise*, Keynes became involved in a series of policy disputes involving business confidence; and as late as summer 1933, Hubert Henderson wrote to him, "You often say, 'It's nonsense to talk about confidence. . . .' "[4] For over three years, while he was at work on both the *Treatise* and *The General Theory*, Keynes was an active opponent of the idea that business confidence was important in the analysis of the Slump.

But then, in the autumn of 1933, after more than three years' controversy, something snapped and Keynes's Michaelmas term lectures were suddenly suffused with confidence. With the introduction of the importance of expected quasi rents to investment, Keynes embraced the position he had been arguing against since the publication of the *Treatise* and used it to "link one thing together with another." In no way was this outcome dictated by the internal logic of the model Keynes was developing; the change in his position can best be understood as a result of his role in many ongoing debates over policy.

"That Is an Extremely Abnormal State of Things?"

During the final stages of the composition of the *Treatise*, Keynes was afforded ample opportunity to rethink the relevance of the confidence tradition in which he had been brought up. Friend and foe alike suggested to him that Britain's economic woes were a direct result of a lack of confidence on the part of businessmen, and that a return to confidence was essential to recovery. But, of course, Keynes was dubious about the importance of a "mythical" force that was thought to somehow be able to turn things around simply on the force of a change in mood. He was now in the thrall of his *Treatise* analysis that explained a Slump by way of an excess of savings over investment, with this

---

3. One of the real problems with Carabelli's (1988), O'Donnell's (1989), and Skidelsky's (1992) accounts is that they do not consider the evolution of Keynes's thinking on the business cycle and confidence. All of these fail to provide an explanation of why Keynes's interest in uncertainty was not manifest in his earlier economic writings; but this is not surprising since none of them note that Keynes's views on uncertainty in his economic writings were undergoing substantial change after 1921. Carabelli, O'Donnell, and Skidelsky each tell a story that depends on Keynes having one unchanged conception of probability after 1921; they then argue that it merely took time for this unchanging conception to become fully integrated into his economics.

4. JMK, xxi, 166. It is exactly this kind of evidence of Keynes's lack of concern with confidence (as late as 1933) that Carabelli's and O'Donnell's accounts fail to address.

disequilibria itself being the result of interest rates being too high; confidence played no integral role.

It seems likely, though, that his strong opposition to confidence arguments in 1930 sprang as much from the conclusion to which they all led as it did from a purely theoretical point. In two cases, the person making the argument came to the conclusion that businessmen's bad nerves made public works, and especially a government budget deficit, a self-defeating move. Keynes had co-authored the rousing plea for the Liberal Party's large-scale public works program, *Can Lloyd George Do It?*, the previous year and he was in no mood now to hear that such programs would not work because they scared businessmen. To him it seemed quite to the contrary; if people were put back to work and began to buy goods, this would increase profits and the increase in profits would revive businessmen's spirits. Instead of seeing confidence as the engine of the system, and something possibly manipulated for its own sake, Keynes reduced confidence to a reflection of the businessmen's actual position. Thus, rather than worrying about businessmen's moods, he believed that one should worry about their bottom lines. If the excess of saving over investment could be eliminated by stimulating state-directed investment, then the economy could be revived and business confidence would follow.[5] Keynes was already predisposed to dismiss confidence as an autonomous force in the economy by virtue of his escape from Marshall and Pigou on this very point, but his determination was all the more resolute given the fact that confidence was now being used not just to explain the trade cycle, but also to argue against activist policies to mitigate it.

It is perhaps ironic that the first person to make a strong confidence argument to Keynes was the co-author of *Can Lloyd George Do It?*, Hubert Henderson. At Keynes's prodding, Henderson had accepted the position of senior civil servant (joint secretary) on the newly formed Economic Advisory Council (E.A.C.) in early 1930, and one of his new responsibilities was to prepare reports for the prime minister, Ramsay MacDonald, on the economic outlook. Keynes, who was a member of the E.A.C., received a copy of Henderson's first report to MacDonald for Keynes's comments.[6] In the report, Henderson expressed a complete volte-face from his position of the previous year; he

---

5. At this point, in 1930, Keynes's argument for public works spending followed from his "special case" argument in the *Treatise;* a nation on the gold standard, incapable of lowering its interest rates, was then justified in undertaking debt-financed public works to stimulate recovery from a slump.

6. Howson and Winch (1977, 25–26) provide the best account of this episode.

emphasized especially that the government's decisions about keeping or rescinding particular taxes and the effect of this on the budget balance would have a direct effect on the economy through their effect on business confidence.[7]

Hubert Henderson to Ramsay MacDonald (draft) 12 March 1930

(5) The British position is further aggravated by the profound and widespread pessimism which prevails today among businessmen, and which is fatal, so long as it continues, to fresh development and enterprise. This again is mainly attributable to the fact that the present slump has supervened on a long period of unsatisfactory trade. But it is aggravated by various special factors, of which the most important is probably general apprehension with regard to the forthcoming Budget, complicated by the uncertainty in regard to the McKenna duties, silk duties, etc. The production of the Budget in mid-April should, therefore, clear the air; but a good deal will depend on whether the actual Budget is from the standpoint of businessmen, worse than or not as bad as vaguely apprehended.

(6) On the other side of the picture, there are various favorable factors, such as the prospect of really cheap money in the fairly near future, none of which, however, seem likely to affect the situation very quickly.

(7) It would be useful, I suggest, to invite opinions from members of the Council as to how the economic [sic] seems likely to develop in the near future, and whether there is anything that could be (done) by you or done by the Government to improve business confidence or otherwise assist the situation.

(Signed) H. D. Henderson

Their election pamphlet did not deal with confidence, but rather relied on the proto-Keynesian idea that the public works expenditures

---

7. A carbon copy of this draft document is deposited in the Keynes Papers, Box EA/1. I have been unable to find a copy of the draft document in the Public Record Office, but Henderson sent a (corrected) copy of the memo directly to MacDonald under his own signature. See Skidelsky 1992, 365, for an argument that Henderson became MacDonald's "favorite economist" at this time; this would apparently account for the private correspondence outside official E.A.C. business. Henderson's note is deposited in PRO 30/69/456.

would raise the level of real economic activity through the increases in income and expenditure of those newly employed; it was very much a mechanical argument. How and why Henderson had changed his tack so quickly is an open question. As a Cambridge economist (who had attended Keynes's lectures), the relevance of confidence would have been a commonplace for him, though not in the form of an argument against public works or deficit spending. Susan Howson and Donald Winch have suggested that Henderson's position in the government, as a civil servant, made him more of an insider than Keynes, and this caused him to be more concerned with purely governmental problems (e.g., budget balance). But while this is clearly true of the widening gap between the two as the 1930s wore on, the initial volte-face is still somewhat of a mystery.[8]

There is no record of Keynes's immediate response to Henderson's memorandum to the prime minister, but the revision of the report for release as the first report of the Committee on Economic Outlook provides an interesting window on Keynes's thinking, since he chaired the committee and the report went out under a covering note by himself and G. D. H. Cole.[9] The revision of the memorandum is most remarkable for the total purging of Henderson's confidence argument. All of the arguments that Henderson had made about the loss of Britain's export markets and the effects of worldwide deflation remained, but the focus on confidence as a separate and distinct element of the problem had disappeared. Confidence remained neither as an explanation of how things had come about or as a part of the consideration of how to engineer recovery. In place of Henderson's concluding suggestion to the prime minister that the key to recovery lay in finding a way to stimulate business confidence, there appeared a version of the list of seven possible remedies for the slump that Keynes was formulating in his other official capacity as a member of the Macmillan Committee. But none of these possible

---

8. See Howson and Winch 1977, 66. Evidence that Henderson had a traditional Cambridge concern with the role of confidence in the business cycle is evidenced by the acknowledgement given to him in the preface to Frederick Lavington's *Trade Cycle* (1922). Lavington's book is a simple restatement of the Marshallian idea that the trade cycle results from swings in business confidence. But while this provides evidence of Henderson's familiarity with confidence arguments it still does not explain his sudden volte-face as regards their relevance to debt-financed public works projects. By highlighting Henderson's work with Richard Hopkins, Peter Clarke (1990) has perhaps helped to explain the suddenness of Henderson's change of mind. To see just how far Henderson strayed one need only consider his 1935 essay, "Do we want Public Works?"

9. For a full account of the release of this first report by the committee, see Howson and Winch 1977, 32.

remedies (cheap money, rationalization, protection, and so on) depended in any way upon a change of mood among businessmen.[10]

We cannot know for sure that it was Keynes who caused these drastic revisions in Henderson's memorandum, but given the vehemence with which Henderson insisted on the importance of confidence six months later when he and Keynes were working together on the Committee of Economists in September and October, it seems most likely that it was Keynes, in his capacity as chair of the Committee on Economic Outlook, who had engineered the changes. Having been overruled once by Keynes, Henderson was not going to let it happen a second time.

Henderson would again attempt to convert Keynes on the importance of confidence two months later in June, but before Henderson's second attempt, Keynes was to encounter the confidence argument at least three more times. These occurred, however, not through his membership on the Economic Advisory Council, but in his capacity as a member of the Macmillan Committee, where he was trying to undercut both the Treasury's opposition to public works and the Bank of England's secretive stance toward bank rate. In spring 1929, the Treasury had worked extensively on developing a critique of the Liberal Party proposal for a large-scale public works scheme, and much of their work made its way into the government's May 1929 White Paper on the Liberal's proposals for large-scale public works.[11] Because of their direct (and improprietous) involvement in the preparation of the document, it provided Keynes with a firsthand opportunity to scrutinize the Treasury view that public works displaced, or crowded out, private investment and, thus, led to no gain in overall employment.[12]

Nine months later, after the Conservatives had been thrown out of office and the new Labour government had created both the Macmillan Committee and the Economic Advisory Council, Keynes was perfectly placed to give the Treasury view a public thrashing; not only was he a member of both groups, he had a clear statement of the Treasury position in the White Paper. Imagine his anticipation, then, in May when the Macmillan Committee called Richard Hopkins, the controller of finance at the Treasury, to testify. Keynes had already presented his own case for public works to the committee in March, and now, two months later, he

---

10. For discussions of Keynes's menu approach to policy recommendations while serving on the Macmillan Committee, see Howson and Winch 1977, 174, and Clarke 1988, chaps. 7 and 8.

11. Clarke 1988, chapter 3, provides the best account of this episode.

12. Keynes responded to the White Paper with a review in *The Nation* on 18 May 1929. This is reprinted in *JMK*, xix, 819–24.

had the civil servant directly answerable for the Treasury view in the dock. Anticipation soon gave way to disappointment, however, as it became obvious that Hopkins was not answering for the crude crowding-out argument. This was immediately obvious in the exchange between the chairman and Hopkins regarding the White Paper and the Treasury view.[13]

> *Hopkins:* I think the Treasury view has sometimes been rather compendiously and not very accurately stated.
> *Macmillan:* Now is your chance, Sir Richard?
> *Hopkins:* If I may say so, officials, if their views are published, start a controversy, and they are not able to intervene in its progress, and sometimes the exact form of their view—
> *Macmillan:* Is a little misunderstood?
> *Hopkins:* —is a little misunderstood.

After Hopkins's long introductory statement, Keynes began his questioning only to find his target moved. When Keynes suggested to Hopkins that he had expected to hear that "any capital that could be found for those schemes would be diverted from other uses," Hopkins replied, "That is much too rigid an expression of any views that have come from us."[14]

What, then, was the basis of the Treasury's objection to large-scale public work schemes?[15] In part, that administrative difficulties made it impossible to bring schemes on-line quickly; in part, that it was difficult to find worthwhile schemes to undertake; and, in part, that the adverse effect of business confidence, if the schemes were viewed as uneconomical, would *cause* additional unemployment. Keynes found it difficult to press too hard against the administrative arguments, but he refused to take the arguments about confidence seriously. Hopkins made it especially difficult to dismiss confidence outright, however, because he continually interjected it as the basis for defining a project as "good" or worthwhile. Keynes, following his predilection to see things from a mechanical perspective, wanted only to know if the expenditure on public works would raise

---

13. The exchange here is from the HMSO Committee on Finance and Industry *Minutes of Evidence* (1931), QQ. 5562–64. The relevant part of Hopkins's appearance is reprinted in *JMK*, xx, 166–79.

14. From the Committee on Finance and Industry *Minutes of Evidence* (1931), Q. 5603.

15. Clarke's (1988, 150–56) account of this episode is excellent, though he draws no connection between this episode and Keynes's later position on confidence. Middleton (1985) also discusses confidence as an element of the changing Treasury view without drawing any connection to the role of confidence in Keynes's later work.

employment (regardless of any psychological effects) and what *formal, numerical* criteria could be enlisted for judging a project; his strategy was not so much to argue against confidence as it was to refuse to recognize it seriously as a part of the argument. But for Hopkins "everything depended on confidence—a consideration now paramount in Treasury thinking."[16]

If Hopkins's testimony, and his use of confidence, came as a surprise to Keynes, it should have been no surprise that two of Keynes's colleagues from Cambridge should introduce confidence in their testimony before the Macmillan Committee. Sandwiched around Hopkins's performance were appearances by Dennis Robertson and Pigou; each insisted on the importance of confidence in restarting the economy.[17] But whether through savvy or monomania, Keynes refused to even acknowledge this part of their concern and pressed ahead with his own idea from the *Treatise* that it was the abnormally high postwar interest rates that were keeping investment from taking place. His exchange with Pigou, which took place the week after Hopkins's testimony, is unusual for his willingness to even make response to the confidence argument, though it is perfectly indicative of his dismissive attitude. In pressing Pigou to say that the high rates of interest required by Britain's adherence to the gold standard led to insufficient investment, Keynes was unable to get complete consent from his prey.[18]

Keynes: Does this not depend on the rate of interest?
Pigou: Undoubtedly, in part.
Keynes: Is not that fundamental?
Pigou: There is the state of mind of the business man. The business man might be in such a state that he would not borrow money or use money at 0 percent.
Keynes: That is an extremely abnormal state of things?
Pigou: It is the two things—interest and his state of mind.

Nor was Keynes of a mood to listen to the confidence argument two days later when from his other roost, on the Economic Advisory Committee, he heard once again from Henderson. Having been dissuaded in March from airing his concern over the effects of the budget on business confidence, Henderson was now more anxious than ever to impress

---

16. Clarke 1988, 151.
17. Robertson's concerns with confidence are evident in QQ. 4832 and 4834 of the Committee on Finance and Industry *Minutes of Evidence.*
18. The following exchanges are QQ. 6613–16 in the Committee on Finance and Industry *Minutes of Evidence.*

upon Keynes the folly of both a large-scale public works scheme and an unbalanced budget. In a long personal letter to Keynes, Henderson began with a cogent argument that a large scheme such as they had endorsed the previous year in *Can Lloyd George Do It?* would become a long-term obligation, making a substantial drain on the budget. He then followed with a related point concerning business confidence.

Hubert Henderson to Keynes 30 May 1930

2. *Psychology*

As regards the importance of psychological factors, I have a strong belief in the following propositions:

(*a*) that where there is no real basis for an alleged psychological influence, I don't believe it is worth considering; but

(*b*) where there are solid grounds for expecting that a certain event will happen, and the grounds are of a kind which the business community can understand, then the results of that event begin to take effect in advance.

Now if you launch a large £200 millions two years' programme, proposing to place £5 millions only on the Budget, there are solid grounds at once for believing that that means that taxation is likely to be increased even higher, year by year, indefinitely; and the business community will certainly take that point. They won't believe that everything will be lovely in the garden in two years' time, and that this programme will be the last: and how, having regard to political realities, can you dispute that their skepticism will be reasonable? It won't therefore merely be a case of their *saying* they're alarmed: they *will be* alarmed. Now really doesn't that matter? I should say the alarm might quite easily serve to counteract fully the employment benefits of the programme, and you would then be in a vicious circle of requiring a still bigger programme, still more unremunerative in character, with an increasing hole in the Budget, and increasing apprehension, until you were faced with either abandoning the whole policy or facing a real panic—flight from the pound and all the rest. I doubt if this is overalarmist.[19]

After a further section on the dangers of "insular socialism," Henderson closed the letter by expressing a fear that Keynes would ignore his argument because it did not gibe with Keynes's political beliefs.

---

19. *JMK*, xx, 358–59.

Hubert Henderson to Keynes 30 May 1930

[Y]ou're over-moved by a sense that it's inconsistent with your self-respect to accept anything savouring of a conservative conclusion. Anyway, don't tell me that my state of mind is shocking. I've abandoned too many orthodoxies now to be moved by that. What are your answers, other than that Balfour and Cadman would agree with me?[20]

Keynes's reply is illustrative in several senses. The bulk of what he says in response revolves around the purely technical questions of whether the public works will increase income and the ultimate impact of this on the budget, which, of course, reflects his very mechanical treatment of economic questions in 1930. His mechanical bent, in turn, leads to his waving off of Henderson's concern with confidence; his response to this as a separate item consists of exactly one sentence: "As regards psychology, I maintain that if I am right that a large capital programme would increase the profits of business men, this would, after the first blush, have more effect on them than anything else."[21] Finally, this brief dismissal embodies the crux of the argument that Keynes would use in dealing with confidence during the next three years; rather than allowing that a change in business psychology could, by itself, cause a change in output or employment, he would talk about the changes that would come about because of his policy proposals and then assert that after these changes had come about confidence would return. This response to Henderson would appear to be the first of his attempts to argue that a return of confidence would *follow from* a recovery rather than lead to one; Keynes was making a mechanical pump-priming argument with no real role for business confidence. Having worked for so many years to develop his Fundamental Equations and to throw off the Cambridge confidence argument, he was not now about to capitulate to those who had not yet liberated themselves, for example, Robertson, Henderson, and Pigou.

It appears that there might have been some change in Keynes's attitude toward confidence in July when he wrote a long and detailed reply to a set of questions that the prime minister had set for all members of the Economic Advisory Council, but his use of confidence in this response seems to have been largely to make his arguments compatible with the

---

20. Ibid.
21. *JMK*, xx, 361.

general tenor of the other advice that MacDonald was receiving.[22] He opens his discussion of the international section with a reference to the "depressed psychology of enterprisers" that would easily have met the approval of a contemporary Treasury mandarin, but he then proceeds to turn the entire argument into a recapitulation of his *Treatise* analysis that interest rates are too high. In the process, he argues that the current situation would hold even if business confidence were not depressed.

At the present time the expectations of new enterprise and new investment as to the returns for which they can hope are below the figure at which lenders will supply them with funds on long term; that is to say there is a gap between the rate of interest asked by lenders and the rate of profit anticipated by enterprisers. This is partly due to a depressed psychology of enterprisers occasioned by the fall of prices and other causes, but much more, in my judgement, to the very high level at which the long-term rate of interest now stands. I doubt whether there has been any period in times of peace during the last hundred years when prudent and legitimate new enterprise would have been able to support the rates of interest now charged. These rates of interest became established as the result partly of the high rates to which the War period accustomed investors; partly of the high rates which it paid enterprisers to incur for the reconstruction of the working capital of the world after the War; partly of the high rates which speculators in "equities" were prepared to pay in Wall Street and elsewhere; and partly of there being a long line of necessitous government borrowers waiting for accommodation, who were prepared to pay almost any rate in order to satisfy their creditors, and were not, in agreeing to pay a given rate of interest, doing so as the result of any calculation that they could employ the money which they were borrowing so as to yield that rate.[23]

Thus, after an auspicious introduction, expectations do not re-enter this part of Keynes's argument and are effectively dismissed as having any real importance in the current circumstances.

Keynes does reintroduce confidence once more in the conclusion of his memo to MacDonald, as the fourth of four ways to help "mak[e] lenders willing to accept a lower rate of interest from home

---

22. The list of questions that the prime minister set for the Council is reprinted in *JMK*, xx, 367.

23. *JMK*, xx, 372.

enterprisers." Reading through to the end of his point, however, reveals a nice ulterior motive for this last-minute insertion of business psychology.

(iv) By promoting a feeling of confidence. The question of confidence, which is of first-class importance in its influence on the investor when he is deciding what terms for home investment are attractive compared with what is offering abroad, is very much tied up with the Budget.

A Budget which involves increased direct taxation would be disastrous in its effect on confidence. Since the yield of the taxes is bound to be disappointing so long as trade, profits and employment are subnormal means that:

(a) all expenditure on new social services, such as pensions, school-leaving and the like, should be ruthlessly postponed until better times;

(b) such moderate economies as are practicable should be searched out, such as remedies for the abuses of the dole;

(c) the one form of new taxation, namely a revenue tariff on manufactured imports which would not have a discouraging effect on industry, shall be favourably regarded; indeed I regard this as essential to a sound Budget in present circumstances.[24]

Keynes was engaged at this time in one of his most spectacular volte-faces, his embrace of tariffs as a short-term remedy for unemployment, and the confidence argument presented him with a perfect way of defending his position.[25] If the Treasury and Henderson were to feed the prime minister a steady diet of confidence, why not use this as a way of arguing for his own pet policies? Keynes could reassure himself that confidence would only follow from the recovery spurred by the revenue tariff, but there was perhaps no harm in couching his argument in his opponents' armor. As Peter Clarke has noted, the political environment at the moment may have convinced Keynes that "a more consensual

---

24. *JMK*, xx, 383.

25. The minor status of Keynes's comments on confidence, when seen in the larger context of his use of his analytical framework from the *Treatise*, is important to remember when one considers Keynes's public statements on tariffs. These statements continued until the spring of 1931; see, for instance, Keynes 1931a. As in his memorandum to MacDonald, however, the statements are always incidental to the main thrust of Keynes's argument. They also all take the form of his effort to make confidence a *reflection* of real conditions, rather than an *autonomous* factor capable of changing those conditions.

approach was needed," and this is certainly consistent with his efforts in the Macmillan Committee at this time to push for any and all of the seven possible remedies he had identified for the Slump.[26] And, of course, he had started the memo anyway with the assertion that high interest rates were "much more" responsible for the Slump than the psychology of businessmen.

In any case, since Keynes's memo to MacDonald was written exactly as he was putting the final touches on the *Treatise,* we know that he could not have been seriously swayed by the confidence argument at this point. If anything, he believed himself to be about to bury the confidence theory of the trade cycle. We can also safely identify his use of confidence in the July memo as an "opportunistic flirtation," given the way in which he was forced to finesse the question of confidence only two months later in the newly formed Committee of Economists.[27]

The Committee of Economists had been set up as a subgroup to report to the E.A.C. in response to a suggestion by Keynes to Ramsay MacDonald in July.[28] Keynes wanted to set a group of economists apart from the union leaders, businessmen and politicians on the E.A.C. to try to form as much of a consensus among "experts" as possible. MacDonald agreed to the attractiveness of the idea and appointed Keynes as chair of a group, which also included Henderson, Pigou, Josiah Stamp, and Lionel Robbins. The group first met in September and hoped to produce a report by late October so that it could be in the hands of the cabinet for the beginning of Parliament.

Keynes had obviously hoped that the consensus to which this group would gravitate would be his own *Treatise* argument, as his self-confidence in his analysis at this point was complete. In May he had told Montagu Norman, the governor of the Bank of England, that he was so sure of his analysis in the *Treatise* that, "I can only say that I am ready to have my head chopped off if it is false," and it was this same self-assurance that led him in July to suggest the creation of the Committee of Econo-

---

26. The risk, and fruitlessness, of pushing for extreme positions at this time would have been evident in Oswald Mosley's recent unsuccessful efforts to push the government to take a firmer stand on mitigating unemployment with new public works projects. His effort ended in his resignation as chancellor of the Duchy of Lancaster. Skidelsky (1967, 165–88) contains the best brief account of Mosley's failure and resignation.

27. The phrase "opportunistic flirtation" comes from Alan Coddington (1982), who used it in quite a different context.

28. Keynes's original letter (dated 10 July 1930) to Ramsay MacDonald suggesting the creation of the Committee of Economists is reproduced in *JMK,* xx, 368–69.

mists.[29] With the final draft of the *Treatise* only four days from completion, his anticipation at the first meeting on 10 September must have been very high indeed.

But in the 14 meetings between then and 24 October, Keynes's hopes were shattered. Of his four companions only Stamp, who was above all interested in pragmatic solutions rather than theoretical controversy, proved to be cooperative. Pigou was noncombative, but there was "a distinct coolness, attributable perhaps to a clash of personal and intellectual styles."[30] Robbins, aged 32, proved the enfant terrible, as he ultimately prepared a formal dissent (over the issue of suggesting a tariff) rather than sign the committee's report. Henderson was willing to go along with the suggestion of a tariff, but he was vociferously opposed to a large-scale public works project and felt that it was "plain as a pikestaff" that money wages needed to be lowered to make British industry more competitive. As regards public works, Henderson repeated his arguments from March and May that the adverse business reaction to a program that would cause long-run budgetary problems would far outweigh any short-run benefits.

> It is utterly wrong under present circumstances to embark on anything in the nature of a gamble, i.e., to pursue policies which one hopes will be beneficial immediately, but will certainly aggravate the situation later on, on the strength of an optimistic assumption that the situation will be much better in a few years time. Moreover, in view of the present condition of business confidence I am very doubtful whether anything which is clearly calculated to make things worse a little later on would yield any immediate advantages on balance.[31]

Likewise, business confidence stood at the crux of Henderson's arguments to the committee for the necessity of lowering monetary wages. In answer to a written question put to the committee by Keynes, "In what way would (*a*) British employment (*b*) British prices (*c*) British real wages be affected by a reduction of British money wages?" Henderson responded that the state of business confidence would determine the outcome.[32]

---

29 JMK, xx, 350–51.
30. Howson and Winch 1977, 64.
31. *JMK,* xx, 452.
32. For the full list of questions that Keynes set for the committee, see *JMK,* xx, 405.

The difficulty in answering this question is that the present precarious state of business confidence may make a great difference to the short period results. Disregarding reactions upon confidence, I am of the opinion that a reduction of British money wages in the relatively high paid industries would tend to aggravate employment immediately by reducing, in the first instance, effective purchasing power, but would tend to improve employment after an interval by improving the competitive position of the unsheltered industries. When, however, account is taken of reactions upon confidence, I am not sure that even the immediate effects of such a reduction would be detrimental to employment, since it would encourage business men to embark on future commitments, of which at present they are very chary.[33]

Nor was Henderson alone in his assessment of the importance of confidence in these two contexts. Two weeks later, in a memorandum of dissent regarding the entire tenor of the committee's work, Robbins sounds little different than Keynes's former co-author. In reference to measures meant to increase the volume of domestic investment, Robbins wrote to the committee, "Nothing is likely to be more efficacious in eliciting such an increase than the restoration of confidence which would follow any move on the part of the Unions to abandon their present wage policy and the more obsolete of their trade customs and restrictions." As regards public works, Robbins was even more eloquent than the mandarins themselves.

Finally the scheme must not be of such nature as to endanger business confidence. It is sad in an official document to have to enter into banalities of this nature, but the calm way in which the recent years it has been assumed that the government could float loans of almost any dimensions for purposes of whatever degree of uselessness without providing a shock to business confidence, suggests that, what in other times would have been a platitude, has now become almost a violent paradox. It is highly questionable whether, *at this stage,* a decision to spend say £200,000,000 on additional road making would not in this way cause more unemployment than it would cure.[34]

But Keynes was undaunted. In the committee's final report, a section was added on business confidence, but Keynes took the authorship

---

33. *JMK*, xx, 452.
34. PRO, Cab. 58/150.

of this section on himself and turned it into a repetition of his own position that confidence, per se, was not an element subject to autonomous movement by the authorities or that moved the economy (apart from the real factors that it reflected).

> The best means of restoring business confidence is a psychological problem on which the opinion of this Committee is not likely to be specially valuable. In the long run we do not see how business confidence is likely to be maintained otherwise than by an actual recovery of business profits. This means that, if business and employment improve for other reasons, the effect of this improvement on business confidence may be cumulative; which is, indeed, a part of the justification of emergency measures of a temporary character. For the effect of judicious emergency measures might be to improve business confidence, after which business confidence might take the place of the emergency measures as providing the necessary stimulus.[35]

A Real Dégringolade

Almost from the beginning, Hubert Henderson's argument with Keynes about confidence had consisted of two prongs. One prong was the *domestic* response of businessmen to the position of the budget; if they were unnerved and foresaw long-term problems, they would get cold feet and enterprise would decline. The second prong was the response to the budget position in the *international* sphere; if foreign-exchange markets responded adversely to the budget position, there would be a loss of confidence in sterling and a "flight from the pound and all the rest."[36] As we know now, it is the first prong of this argument that ultimately animated *The General Theory*. In retrospect, however, it would seem that it was the second prong that brought Keynes around to the real significance of confidence in macroeconomic analysis.

Initially, Keynes was completely unsympathetic to Henderson's argument about a crisis in sterling. In the months following Henderson's warning (May 1930) he in fact seems to have taunted Henderson about his fears, for in October when Henderson was trying to convince the Committee of Economists that under Keynes's tutelage they were evad-

---

35. PRO, Cab. 58/151, EAC(H) 127, 24 October 1930, ¶56.
36. *JMK,* xx, 359.

ing the necessity of recommending wage cuts across the board, Keynes's persistence became a part of Henderson's memo to the committee.

The only ground on which the policy of evasion appears to be justified is, as I have said, the expression of a hope that, if we put off the evil day a little longer, something will turn up after all. But I don't think that Keynes is really very confident of that; and from a question he has put to me more than once in the course of the discussions, I fancy the difference between us is really of another character. He has asked me whether it would really matter so very much if there was a flight from the pound, and a real *dégringolade* of British currency and credit.[37]

But Keynes remained unconvinced. Even in early 1931 he was writing to his friend, the American investment banker Walter Case, that the talk of a crisis was "complete moonshine."[38] Henderson, of course, proved to be the more prescient as regards a crisis and Britain was finally forced off the gold standard in September.

Keynes's immediate response, however, was not to embrace Henderson's argument. Far from it. Keynes was happy to have the country untied from gold and the restrictions it put upon policy makers and so, rather than acquiescing in retrospective hand wringing over how more attention to economizing and the budget might have saved the day and kept Britain on gold, his concern raced ahead to how to manage the new position.[39]

But despite the fact that his concerns raced away from Henderson's, Keynes nonetheless found himself face-to-face with confidence. In the most obvious sense, this arose in the popular terminology for what had just happened: a crisis in confidence. Keynes, for instance, quickly adopted an insider's explanation of the crisis in his essays and speeches. "The 'margins' as we call them, upon confidence in the maintenance of which the debt and credit structure of the modern world depends, have 'run off.' "[40] There was no way to avoid the fact that confidence really had played a role in what had happened.

In some sense, however, Keynes could accommodate this in his previous approach to confidence; just as business confidence was taken

---

37. *JMK*, xx, 453.
38. *JMK*, xx, 486.
39. It was at this point that Keynes abandoned his advocacy of tariffs. With the abandonment of the gold standard, the basis for his argument in favor of tariffs was removed.
40. *JMK*, xxi, 39–40.

to be a reflection of bottom lines, the confidence of those who were liquidating their sterling holdings in September 1931 was a reflection of the currency's actual position.[41] This kind of continued adherence to his older framework was manifest in July 1931 when he spoke of his "scientific theory of booms and busts" while continuing to argue from his *Treatise* position. Thus, his first "turn" to the rhetoric of confidence may not have evidenced any significant change in his position.

Quickly, however, he found himself even further involved with confidence and this, again, directly as a result of Britain's new financial position. Keynes was frantically searching for a policy to avoid further financial crisis and more generally for a monetary policy to return the country to stability.[42] But the more he looked, the more he found that the authorities were bound by the expectations of bondholders and money managers. Slowly a perception was building in Keynes that confidence played a role in financial markets that really might not reflect anything other than the psychology of the participants.[43]

The first unambiguous evidence of this change would seem to be in Keynes's comments on the Treasury's 1932 Conversion Scheme for over £2 billion of 5 percent War Loan (1939–47) to a 3-1/2 percent War Loan (1952 or later). On 18 July 1932, he prepared a memorandum on the scheme for the Committee on Economic Information and this appeared in a slightly revised form in the next issue of the *Economic Journal*. The new

---

41. In an article published in *The Sunday Express* a week after the abandonment of the gold standard, this is exactly Keynes's position. He claims that sterling was overvalued and that going off the gold standard was "unavoidable" for that reason. He never mentions the abandonment of the gold standard as being the result of abnormal psychology or incorrect expectations. In fact, in talking about the process by which sterling's exchange value will be determined in the new circumstances, he dismisses the effects of optimism and pessimism and argues that "The equilibrium value of sterling is the same as it was a month ago" (*JMK,* ix, 246–47). Moggridge (1972, 236) argues in a similar vein that even in the absence of the liquidity crisis in the summer of 1931, the underlying fundamentals would have made it difficult to avoid suspension of gold convertibility.

42. As opposed to the literature in economic history, it is not usually recognized in the literature in the history of economic thought that Keynes's policy proposals in the 1930s changed in response to changing circumstances. See above, note 27.

43. Don Moggridge has pointed out to me that Keynes's personal experience as an investor and speculator may have influenced his views on financial markets. This is undoubtedly the case, as a careful study of his investment activity (such as Moggridge's in *JMK,* xii, 1–113) shows that he gained, and lost, several fortunes on the changing winds of market psychology. In the case being discussed here, this might be most obvious in Keynes's actions with the investment portfolio of the Provincial Insurance Company in 1931–32. As Oliver Westall (1992) has shown, Keynes moved the Provincial heavily into consuls in anticipation of a fall in interest rates.

freedom provided by the abandonment of the gold standard did not point to a set of mechanistic forces driving the financial markets or to mechanistic policy solutions. Under the gold standard, the domestic rate(s) of interest would have been very narrowly dictated by Britain's economic circumstances vis-à-vis the rest of world. Now the domestic rate(s) had no firm anchor in these circumstances. The problem was not just for the authorities, however, for Keynes realized that everyone in the financial markets was unclear about where rates could, or should, be.

Popular opinion in relation to the conversion is, as I interpret it, a peculiar combination such as could only exist, perhaps, in this country, of a keen desire to make the scheme an overwhelming success, both by personal and by communal action, with an unspoken conviction or at least a suspicion that the whole thing is in truth a bit of bluff which a fortunate conjunction of circumstances is enabling us to put over ourselves and one another, and that the new War Loan may be expected to fall to a discount in due course.

I am not sure that the authorities themselves are entirely free from an idea of this kind. Nevertheless I plead for a policy based on the opposite hypothesis. For I am convinced that the conversion scheme is anything but a bluff. A great reduction in the long-term rate of interest corresponds profoundly to the character and, indeed, to the necessities of the underlying facts, and it may even be a necessary condition of the survival of the existing financial structure of society. Nor is there anything in the attendant circumstances which need prevent our achieving it. But it will not happen by itself and must be pursued with deliberate purpose. For there is a large conventional or psychological element in the market rate of interest which needs firm and skilful management.[44]

This shifting concern with the influence of opinion on interest rates is also clearly evident in Keynes's 1932 lectures at Cambridge. During the Easter term he had given a set of lectures in place of the ones he had postponed the previous Michaelmas term while he contemplated the problems with the *Treatise*. The remains of these spring lectures indicate very rudimentary efforts to work out the inconsistencies and problems of the *Treatise* but are very much in the same spirit. The Michaelmas term lectures, however, represent several significant departures, the most striking of which is his conversion to the idea that there is difference

---

44. *JMK*, xxi, 116–17.

between a "money economy" and a "monetary economy"; the former involves the use of money as a neutral means of facilitating trade, whereas the latter is an economy "in which money affects motives and decisions so that monetary policy in the short and long run is essential to prognostication."[45] This striking departure leads Keynes to another: the systematic treatment of uncertainty *in financial markets*. As per his policy interest in what forces might effect the success of the Conversion Scheme, Keynes is now interested in the theoretical impact of uncertainty on financial markets. Rather than an ad hoc treatment meant to facilitate a digression, however, his interest in uncertainty is now central to his argument about why agents hold money and/or bonds. "Liquidity preference is not an expression of time preference, rather it is more an expression of expectations."[46]

But Keynes's argument of this point neither releases him completely from his *Treatise* mentality, nor puts him squarely within the framework of *The General Theory*.[47] As regards *The General Theory*, Keynes had yet to consider uncertainty in the context of investment or effective demand (indeed, had not yet invented effective demand!) and so had not introduced his concern across his whole analytical model. As regards the *Treatise*, the introduction of expectations to the financial markets marked neither a general concern with confidence nor an abandonment of his mechanical approach to policy making.[48] The extent of his concern with the problem of uncertainty as well as his residual, mechanical approach to policy are evident in his proposed solution to the problem in a piece that appeared on Christmas Eve 1932 on the impending World Economic Conference.

The trouble began with something which is best described as "a state of financial tension." In the United States the causes of the tension were internal; elsewhere they were in their origins mainly

---

45. Keynes changed the title of his lectures for the Michaelmas term to reflect this substantive change in his argument. Whereas the lectures had been titled "The Pure Theory of Money" in the Easter term, they were now "The Monetary Theory of Production."

46. In Rymes 1989, 68.

47. Both Patinkin (1976) and Milgate (1982) concur that Keynes was poised at this point between the *Treatise* and *The General Theory*. Clarke (1988, 263) would seem to have correctly identified the summer of 1932 as the moment of the birth of effective demand.

48. The word *confidence* did not enter Keynes's argument in the *Treatise*. Certainly his many policy suggestions in the Macmillan Committee were based on a straightforward mechanistic analysis following from the Fundamental Equations.

international. These initiating causes are well known—on the one hand a frenzy of speculation in the United States, on the other hand a cessation of the international lending which had been off-setting the disequilibrium of the balances of payment between countries which War debts and tariffs would have already produced otherwise. A state of financial tension means that individuals and communities suddenly find much increased difficulty in putting their hands on money to meet their obligations, with the result that they take various measures to reduce their purchasing. Others, not actually in difficulty, fear that the same thing may overtake them later, and from precaution reduce their purchasing also. The reduced demand, which is the same thing as reduced purchasing, causes prices to fall; the fall of prices diminishes profits; and the entrepreneurs of the world, whether they are in difficulties or not, have a diminished incentive to produce output or to make the purchases and create the incomes which would have accompanied it. Thus the declines in demand, in prices, in profits, in output and in incomes feed on themselves and one another.

When financial tension leads to a diminution in demand, the decline necessarily feeds on itself, because each step which an individual (or a community) takes to protect himself and to relieve his own tension merely has the effect of transferring the tension to his neighbour and of aggravating his neighbour's distress. The course of exchange, as we all know, moves round a closed circle. When we transmit the tension, which is beyond our own endurance, to our neighbour, it is only a question of a little time before it reaches ourselves again travelling round the circle.

There is one, and only one, genuine remedy; namely, to increase demand—in other words to increase expenditure. As the slump progresses, it becomes more difficult to do this. At first a relief in the financial tension would have been enough by itself. But when the decline of prices and profits has gone beyond a certain point, the incentive to produce, and not merely the financial ability, has disappeared. At this point, the state itself must, in my judgement, start the ball rolling by deliberately organizing expenditure.[49]

Keynes had advocated public works and loan expenditure in the *Treatise* only in the special case of a country on the gold standard that

49. *JMK*, xxi, 212–13.

could not lower interest rates; now he was prepared to advocate them for a country off the gold standard and faced with "financial tension." But although his lectures at the time indicate that he saw the uncertainty that created this tension in the financial markets as fundamental, rather than ad hoc, his solution to the problem was unchanged. If money managers were uncertain and paralyzed, the government certainly should not be!

Keynes's lingering magic formula mentality is best seen in his *Means to Prosperity*, which was published three months later. Here Keynes makes his second great, impassioned appeal for public works, and he does it using a variant of Kahn's multiplier. But it was exactly his adherence to this mechanical approach that drew Hubert Henderson back to his comments of three years earlier. Henderson was unconvinced by Keynes's use of the multiplier—"I don't like the approach of the Kahn calculations"—and his ultimate reason for this was business confidence.

H. D. Henderson to J. M. Keynes 28 February 1933

This brings me to my second main qualification of the calculations. This is the familiar one that the public works schemes may in various ways, e.g., by raising rates of interest, disturbing confidence, etc., diminish the volume of general industrial activity. In present conditions I don't think this point has any force as regards a moderate unostentatious programme: but it seems to me to have real force if it were a question of a splash grandiose programme, and in that connection the points I have made in the preceding two paragraphs are highly pertinent. You often say—"It's nonsense to talk about confidence; confidence depends on orders." Very likely. But I maintain that if you were to announce that you were going in for a large £200 million programme, you would not get a single order under that programme for at least a year, whereas the effects on the gilt-edged market and the like of the announcement of your intention would be immediate. You might thus easily get a vicious circle wound up before your virtuous circle had begun to operate at all. Speaking generally, therefore, I am very much off the idea of public works as a major constructive remedy for our present troubles.[50]

Thus, while Keynes had been jarred by the reality of the importance of confidence in one prong of Hendersons's arguments (i.e., international) and this had begun to lead him to a broader consideration of the

---

50. *JMK*, xxi, 166.

role of expectations in domestic financial markets, the other prong (i.e., domestic business expectations) was still of virtually no concern to him. The Michaelmas 1932 lectures make this clear, for while investment and the inducements to invest play a role in several of the lectures, the description of these inducements is always in terms perfectly compatible with what is said in the *Treatise*. Perhaps the best evidence of this lies in the third lecture, where Keynes talks throughout of the effect of inequalities between investment and saving, the hallmark of the *Treatise,* without ever attempting a description of fundamental uncertainty as effecting investment. In fact, profits (Q) are given exactly the same definition as in the *Treatise:*

$$Q = I - S.$$

Keynes does speak of "the expectation of quasi-rent" in lectures five, six, and seven, but he does not imbue the term with other than the most literal meaning—what investors reasonably expect to receive in return for their investment. The fact that these expectations are essentially a reflection of the real position of the investors is captured well in the seventh lecture (21 November 1932).

> If one is dealing with the short period, it is unlikely that B (the expectation of quasi-rents) will be much affected by the amount of current output. But, during a boom, for example, the output of capital assets may lead to a diminuation in the expectation of quasi-rents, other things remaining equal.[51]

Thus, while he refers to expectations of quasi rents as a "fundamental factor of market psychology"[52] in the sixth lecture, he does not suggest by this that the minds of businessmen are determined by their moods or anything other than their *real* positions. Having capitulated to Ramsey on the question of the existence of logical relations, it was axiomatic that any expectation was "psychological," but Keynes did not yet seem to believe that the minds of businessmen were far from the facts at hand.

And, of course, any doubt about the status of uncertainty in Keynes's thought at this time must be quelled by the mechanistic certainty of *The Means to Prosperity*. In public, where he was attempting to

---

51. In Rymes 1989, 79.
52. Ibid., 76.

use Kahn's multiplier to present a state-of-the-art argument, there was no mention of uncertainty or expectations at all. Likewise, Henderson's comment in response to *The Means*—"You often say it is nonsense to talk about confidence . . ."—would indicate no significant turn in Keynes's thinking by the spring of 1933.

The fall of 1933 marks the real watershed in Keynes's thinking on uncertainty. Now, for the first time, he employed expectations in the whole panoply of ways that characterize the *General Theory*.[53] In particular, expectations now played a role in financial markets through liquidity preference; a role in investment through "prospective quasi-rents [which] are very fluctuating things"; and a role in the level of employment through entrepreneurs' expectation of income. Corresponding to the first two of these uses, Keynes developed his idea of long-term expectations; corresponding to the last, he developed his idea of short-term expectations. Everything that is fundamental about uncertainty was now in place.

But how had this change come about? How had the man who called confidence as an important element in the Great Depression "nonsense" come to the point of making it a centerpiece in his theoretical arguments? What had happened between February 1933 and the Michaelmas term? The most obvious place to start would seem to be Hubert Henderson's three-year campaign to convert Keynes back to confidence. Although many people—Hopkins, Robertson, Pigou, Henderson, and Robbins—had attempted to get Keynes's attention on this point in 1930, apparently only Henderson continued to pursue the point over the entire three years that it took for Keynes to change his mind. But even if we cannot be sure of the particular person(s) who helped convert Keynes to confidence, it seems impossible to imagine that his long experience of confidence arguments *in the policy world* did not affect their introduction to his theoretical model. And even if one could discount the history of his experience with confidence arguments, one cannot neglect the effect of the dégringolade in 1931 and the changes that it brought about in Keynes's theoretical treatment of the financial markets. For certainly it is unreasonable to think that the development of his ideas on liquidity preference with their strong dependence on confidence were not a part of the wider development of his thinking on uncertainty.

Thus, it seems impossible to escape the conclusion that the central

---

53. It is exactly this point that Clarke (1988, 303) misses when he argues that confidence was introduced into *The General Theory* in 1935 as an afterthought rather than as an integral part of the book.

role of uncertainty in *The General Theory* arose from the *external* influence of his concern with financial markets and economic policy. Although Ramsey had convinced him to abandon his earlier rationalistic conception of probability, that had not been enough, by itself, to bring uncertainty to the center of his economic analysis.[54]

The Monetary Theory of Production

If Keynes's concern with confidence was externally determined or externally influenced by the importance of uncertainty in financial markets or investment decisions, it was not the case that its impact came solely in his models of those parts of the economy. To be sure, uncertainty entered in a new and important way into the liquidity preference function in Michaelmas 1932 and in expected quasi rents in Michaelmas 1933, but something even more fundamental was happening than these particular innovations. The larger sense of what was happening is best captured in the change in the title of his lectures between autumn 1932 and autumn 1933. The course of lectures had been titled "The Pure Theory of Money"; now they became "The Monetary Theory of Production."

In the literal sense, of course, this was meant to capture the attempt on Keynes's part to correct the problems in the *Treatise* that had arisen from his tacit assumption that output was fixed. But Keynes imbued the switch in titles with even more significance than the attempt to model changes in output.[55] In his contribution to a festschrift for Arthur Spiethoff that bears the same new title as his lectures, Keynes explained that he had a completely new conception of what monetary economics entail.

In my opinion the main reason why the problem of crises is unsolved, or at any rate why this theory is so unsatisfactory, is to be found in the lack of what might be termed a monetary theory of production.

The theory which I desiderate would deal, in contradistinction to this, with an economy in which money plays a part of its own and affects motives and decisions and is, in short, one of the operative fac-

---

54. Perhaps it is because Clarke (1988) does not identify uncertainty as crucial to *The General Theory* that he minimizes the role of external influences in the book's construction.

55. Keynes's first work under this title is reprinted in *JMK*, xiii, 408–11. It is largely an attempt to define what he means by the phrase.

tors in the situation, so that the course of events cannot be predicted, either in the long period or in the short, without a knowledge of the behavior of money between the first state and the last. And it is this which we ought to mean when we speak of a monetary economy.[56]

Thus it is not just that he needed or wanted a theory of output, but that he believed that monetary economics dealt with how economic motives and decisions, in general, were affected by the existence of money.[57]

The crux of Keynes's insight was that uncertainty influenced *all* decisions in a monetary economy. He recognized this common thread in each of the economic behaviors he analyzed. The decision to hold cash was a matter of uncertainty about the future of bond prices and asset values; the decision to invest involved uncertainty about future profits; the decision to consume involved uncertainty over future income; and the decision to hire workers involved uncertainty over future demand for the goods they would produce. Suddenly, from the seeds of his observations about the difficulties of controlling interest rates after the abandonment of the gold standard, it became clear that everyone's actions in a monetary economy were influenced by their confidence (or lack of it) in the future.

The word *confidence* first appears to enter Keynes's lectures and notes in mid-1934 in the draft table of contents for his first page proofs of *The General Theory,* "Chapter 12: The state of long-term expectations (or confidence)" (which survives with virtually no changes into the final edition). The pervasiveness of uncertainty across his entire model is most clear in his mid-1934 draft of chapter 9, "The functions relating employment, consumption and investment." Here he formally articulates his model of effective demand and gives expectations a dual role. The effective demand function, $F(N)$, consists of two components, consumption and investment, and each of these is in turn a function of E, the state of long-term expectation. Thus he gives

---

56. *JMK*, xiii, 408–9.

57. Post-Keynesians have focused extensively on Keynes's interest in expectations and the connection of this interest to his conception of money's role in the economy. Roy Rotheim (1981) is an excellent example. By some queer inversion, however, they have largely taken this as representing the basis for an argument on Keynes's part that economic theorizing is a futile activity. See, for example, Paul Davidson 1991. Prima facie this is an incredible conclusion given that the insight led to Keynes's greatest theoretical success. Allan Meltzer (1988, 280–85) and Don Patinkin (1990, 217–19) offer cogent critiques of the Post-Keynesian interpretation of Keynes.

$$C = f_1(N, r, E)$$
$$I = f_2(N, r, E)$$
$$F(N) = f_1 (N, r, E) + f_2(N, r, E)$$

where N is the level of employment and r is the interest rate.[58] Expectations enter in yet another form, however, in that both f_1 and f_2 are themselves expected quantities; when entrepreneurs make their employment decisions they are *anticipating* the amount of consumption and investment expenditure that will eventuate.

Each of these individual functions existed in Keynes's drafts and lectures before 1934, but never had they been pulled together in this fashion around the central pivot of expectations.

In its final form, *The General Theory* did not contain the explicit functional forms that Keynes used in this first set of page proofs, but the argument was unchanged. Chapters 3 and 5 present effective demand as consisting of the expectation of consumption and investment for the period. Chapter 12 presents Keynes's theory of the state of long-term expectation, or confidence, and its effect on investment. And outside the loop of effective demand proper, but the first to have been developed, are the theories of liquidity preference and the rate of interest in chapters 13 and 15. The tenor of Keynes's Michaelmas 1933 lectures would suggest that this final form of his model was in place by then.[59] All the pieces except the marginal efficiency of capital were in place by late 1932 and then, with the full articulation of this concept, he seems to have linked one thing together with another sometime around Christmas 1933. The strictly textual evidence, in any case, cements this date as no later than mid-1934. Although he was to title his book *The General Theory of Employment, Interest, and Money* in an apparent attempt to make his work look larger in scope than (and to entail) the classical theory, Keynes really had been successful at constructing a *monetary theory of production* in the sense in which he meant it. His years of arguing against confidence in the world of policy had culminated in a macroeconomic model suffused with uncertainty.

---

58. In his formal explication of these equations (*JMK,* 13, 441–42), Keynes does allow that it "may sometimes be legitimate" to omit interest rates and expectations from C_1.

59. Patinkin (1976, 79) has noted the direct parallelism between the student notes from the Michaelmas term lectures in 1933 and the formal presentation of Keynes's model in his 1934 draft.

"I Fancy One Has to Tackle It on the Basis of 'Equivalent Certainties' "

But what are we to make of this monetary theory of production? Was the reintroduction of uncertainty to Cambridge monetary theory really a revolution? Was Keynes's concern with uncertainty, expectations, and confidence just a "prescientific" vision that had no concrete analogue in his "scientific" constructs?[60] Referring to both Keynes's book and a 1937 essay in which he recapitulated his main points and laid particular stress upon the role of uncertainty, Don Patinkin has said, "In neither the *General Theory* nor the 1937 article in the *Quarterly Journal of Economics* . . . does Keynes develop a theory of economic behavior under uncertainty."[61] Is it, then, the case that Keynes's monetary theory of production led to new and revolutionary theoretical construct(s), such as effective demand, but that he made no theoretical use of uncertainty?

On its face, Patinkin's claim seems incredible. After all, we know from the lectures and drafts that each and every theoretical construct in *The General Theory* was explicitly formed in terms of expectations. Liquidity preference is "an expression of expectations" and hence so is the rate of interest. Expectations enter formally into the articulation of both the propensity to consume and the marginal efficiency of capital. Effective demand, and aggregate supply, are both defined in terms of the expectation of consumption and investment. And, last but not least, from no later than mid-1934 Keynes was formally representing these different expectation-determined functions together as a whole in what was to become the chapter of *The General Theory* entitled "Expectation as Determining Output and Employment." Given all this, together with what Keynes said during the construction of his book about the need to construct a theory that incorporated money's effect upon motivations and decisions and afterward about the central role of uncertainty, it seems impossible to say that Keynes had not developed "a theory of economic behavior under uncertainty."

But Patinkin's criterion regarding what constitutes such a theory is a very narrow one, for while he does not discuss all of Keynes's uses of expectation, he does explicitly acknowledge Keynes's intention

---

60. The argument that one can separate "prescientific" vision from analytical constructs is, of course, Joseph Schumpeter's (1954).

61. Patinkin's (1976, 142) assertion here is really just a repeat of Samuelson's (1946) canard in his obituary of Keynes (as Patinkin notes).

to model uncertainty in the functions for liquidity preference and investment.

In order to place things in their proper perspective, let me also remind the reader that the nonprobabilistic nature of economic uncertainty which Keynes emphasized in both these writings had been emphasized long before by Frank Knight in his classic *Risk, Uncertainty, and Profit* (1921). Let me also point out that Keynes does not really make much analytical use of this uncertainty. Thus, as already indicated, the only operational conclusions that he bases on it are the relatively general ones that (*a*) there is a speculative demand for money which depends inversely on the rate of interest (a conclusion which in large part Keynes had already reached in the *Treatise*) and (*b*) there are wide fluctuations in the volume of investment, and this in turn is one of the major causes of the business cycle (a proposition which had been a commonplace for students of the cycle for many years). In neither the *General Theory* nor the 1937 article in the *Quarterly Journal of Economics*, however does Keynes develop a theory of economic behavior under uncertainty.[62]

Two related points in this statement help to elucidate Patinkin's criteria for a "theory of economic behavior under uncertainty." One is that the fact that a function exists by virtue of an agent's uncertainty does *not* mean that it constitutes a theory of economic behavior under uncertainty. The second is that Keynes's theory is "nonprobabilistic." Together these two points appear to suggest that the criterion for a theory of economic behavior under uncertainty is that it be probabilistic and that it include some formal calculus for the representation of this probabilistic theory. Thus, the narrow criterion that Patinkin employs would appear to be something like a Bayesian model of decision making in the axiomatized system that Leonard Savage presented in *The Foundations of Statistics;* had Keynes introduced something like this, he would have made "analytical use" of his vision that uncertainty is crucial to behavior in a monetary economy.[63]

Such a narrow criterion seems ahistorical, however, and thus seems to obscure both Keynes's analytical intent and his achievement. To be sure, Keynes did not attempt to employ the type of model that Patinkin

---

62. Patinkin 1976, 141–42.
63. For a similar argument from a different direction see Davidson 1991.

suggests would define a theory of economic behavior under uncertainty. But it can quite reasonably be shown that Keynes's method of modeling expectations was both probabilistic and state of the art.

To make this argument perfectly clear, it seems best to repeat that Keynes did not conceive of a theory of decision making under uncertainty as mathematically complete or sophisticated as the ideal-type in Patinkin's argument. That is, he conceived neither a formal mathematical theory for how new information is used to revise probabilities, nor a formal, axiomatized decision theory. As regards the first of these, Keynes explicitly denied the validity of Bayesian inference in *Probability* and there is no extant evidence that he ever changed his mind on this point.[64] As regards the second, it should be remembered exactly how Keynes envisaged that agents formed their expectations. In both *The General Theory* and the *Quarterly Journal of Economics* article, Keynes makes it perfectly clear that agents form their expectation by means of a *social convention*. In *The General Theory* he suggests only one convention, but in the *Quarterly Journal* he expands this into three separate points.

> In practice we have tacitly agreed, as a rule, to fall back on what is, in truth, a *convention*. The essence of this convention—though it does not, of course, work out quite so simply—lies in assuming that the existing state of affairs will continue indefinitely, except in so far as we have specific reasons to expect a change. This does not mean that we really believe that the existing state of affairs will continue indefinitely. We know from extensive experience that this is most unlikely. The actual results of an investment over a long term of years very seldom agree with the initial expectation.[65]
>
> How do we manage in such circumstances to behave in a manner which saves our faces as rational, economic men? We have devised for the purpose a variety of techniques, of which much the most important are the three following:
>
> (1) We assume that the present is a much more serviceable guide to the future than a candid examination of past experience would show it to have been hitherto. In other words we largely ignore the prospect of future changes about the actual character of which we know nothing.

---

64. See my article (Bateman 1990) for a discussion of Keynes's views on induction.
65. *JMK*, vii, 152.

(2) We assume that the *existing* state of opinion as expressed in prices and the character of existing output is based on a *correct* summing up of future prospects, so that we can accept it as such unless and until something new and relevant comes into the picture.

(3) Knowing that our own individual judgement is worthless, we endeavor to fall back on the judgement of the rest of the world which is perhaps better informed. That is, we endeavor to conform with the behavior of the majority of the average. The psychology of a society of individuals each of whom is endeavoring to copy the others leads to what we may strictly term a *conventional* judgement.[66]

But in each case, the argument comes to the same thing. The idea that people form their expectations on the basis of such conventions first appeared in the Michaelmas 1933 lectures at the point that Keynes was extending the influence of uncertainty to expected quasi rents; he never abandoned it.

To return to the question at hand, however, we need to ask whether this insight was translated into anything like a theory of economic behavior under uncertainty. Did Keynes do anything (analytically) with his insight? A reasonable reader might say, "Why, of course he did, every major function in the book is explicitly concerned with uncertainty." But there is more to Keynes's achievement than this. For while he can legitimately be claimed to have been the first person to build an interconnected model of aggregate activity that could analytically explain macroeconomic fluctuations, he was, at the same time, the first to introduce an analytical treatment of intersubjective probability. If we can believe Keynes, of course, we know that he acquiesced to Ramsey's devastating critique of *Probability*'s central argument that probabilities are objective, Platonic entities; it remains to be shown that Keynes intended to represent his agents' beliefs via an extension of Ramsey's subjective probabilities as being determined intersubjectively by social conventions.

The first brush with expectations in *The General Theory* would seem to give an unambiguous answer. In constructing his model of effective demand, Keynes gives a direct explanation of agents calculating expected values on the basis of the possible outcomes and their respective probabilities.

66. *JMK*, xiv, 114.

An entrepreneur, who has to reach a practical decision as to his scale of production, does not, of course, entertain a single undoubting expectation of what the sale-proceeds of a given output will be, but several hypothetical expectations held with varying degrees of probability and definiteness. By his expectation of proceeds I mean, therefore, that expectation of proceeds which, if it were held with certainty, would lead to the same behaviour as does the bundle of vague and more various possibilities which actually makes up his state of expectation when he reaches his decision.[67]

One may protest that his explanation is less felicitous here than it was in the *Tract* (see chap. 4, "Calculating on a Probability"), but Keynes was apparently quite satisfied with it as this passage first appeared in the 1934 page proofs and survived untouched into the final text.[68] In introducing his reader to chapter 5 (Expectation as Determining Output and Employment), he confidently referred back to this passage as the explanation of what he meant by expectation.

Keynes made a distinction, of course, between short-term and long-term expectations, and since this treatment of effective demand involves only short-term expectations it might be protested that he did not mean to represent long-term expectations in the same way. His correspondence, however, both before and after the publication, indicates exactly the opposite. The first evidence of this comes from his response in 1935 to a paper by Robert Bryce, who had been sitting in on the Michaelmas lectures for three years. Bryce had written up his own version of Keynes's theory and presented it in four sessions at Hayek's monetary seminar at the London School of Economics and had sent a copy to Keynes. In his discussion of investment, Bryce says, "Due allowance must be made here both for risk, i.e., the mathematical expectation of the return must be used, and also for uncertainty and the cost of bearing it."[69]

In reply, Keynes praised the paper: "I think it is excellently done, and I am astonished that you have been able to give so comparatively complete a story within so short a space."[70] Keynes offered no criticism or dissent.

---

67. *JMK*, vii, 24.
68. *JMK*, xiv, 370–71.
69. The notes for Bryce's lectures at LSE are deposited in the Keynes Papers. They are reprinted in *JMK*, xxix, 132–50. The passage cited here is from p. 139.
70. *JMK*, xxix, 150.

Keynes returned to the point in a more substantive and direct way in 1938 in correspondence with another former pupil, Hugh Townshend. Townshend was himself writing about uncertainty in economic behavior by this time and he had instigated a correspondence with Keynes on the point.

J. M. K. to H. Townshend 27 July 1938

The matter you are tackling is a very important and interesting one often in my mind. But the enclosed treatment seems to me still too much half-baked. I fancy one has to tackle it on the basis of "equivalent certainties."[71]

Townshend, in response, considered several problems that arise from trying to employ these equivalent certainties. Keynes's response was warm and encouraging.

J. M. K. to H. Townshend 7 December 1938

I am interested that you are still pursuing the elusive problems discussed in your letter of November 25th. There is very little in that letter from which I want to differ.[72]

Thus, from the evidence both before and after the publication of *The General Theory*, it seems that Keynes had in mind the representation of probabilities in the guise of "equivalent certainties," or the weighted average of each potential outcome by its probability. He may have minimized his use of them in accordance with his general effort to make the presentation in the book as nonmathematical as possible, but he appears by all accounts to have meant what he said when he first introduced the concept in chapter 3.

"Fluffy Gray Lumps"

After making the argument that Keynes's treatment of uncertainty in *The General Theory* is both probabilistic and analytical, it is nonetheless necessary to qualify this conclusion in order to insure that the full nature of Keynes's work is not misunderstood. At least two types

---

71. *JMK*, xxix, 288–89.
72. Ibid., 293.

of misunderstanding or misinterpretation seem possible. One would be that since Keynes was employing probabilities and equivalent certainties, then his treatment of uncertainty is perfectly equivalent to more modern treatments, virtually all of which start with the same building blocks.[73] Another possible misunderstanding would be that since "all Keynes was doing" was multiplying outcomes by their probabilities, then he was not really doing anything revolutionary or pathbreaking.

Perhaps the easiest way to see the necessary qualification to the story of Keynes's use of probability is to go back to his correspondence with Townshend. Following his admonition to Townshend that "one has to tackle it on the basis of 'equivalent certainties' " he goes on to discuss the problem of whether or not probabilities are numerical (an obvious problem should they not be).

J. M. K. to H. Townshend 27 July 1938

Moreover the economic problem is, of course, only a particular department of the general principles of conduct, although particularly striking in this connection because it seems to bring in numerical estimations by some system of arranging alternative decisions in order of preference, some of which will provide a norm by being numerical. But that still leaves millions of cases over where one cannot even arrange an order of preference. When all is said and done, there is an arbitrary element in the situation.[74]

Taken literally, this means that there are cases in which people actually can (and do) make the calculations represented by equivalent certainties, while at other times *an equivalent certainty is merely a heuristic to represent a decision that had been made on other grounds.* In the latter case, one would be using an equivalent certainty to represent the probabilities *implicit* in a decision in which they had not really played any *explicit* role.[75] The theorist is clearly in an anomalous position if this

---

73. An example of this kind of reasoning (i.e., equating Keynes's approach to the modern use of mathematical expectation) is found in Meltzer's book, *Keynes's Monetary Theory* (1988).

74. *JMK,* xxix, 289.

75. This is exactly the way that Ramsey argues about probability in his paper "Truth and Probability" (1931). He argues that probabilities may be implicit in people's actions, though not explicit in their decisions to act.

latter case holds, for the analytical constructs have no analogues in reality.[76] Nor is this latter case a rare one.

J. M. K. to H. Townshend 7 December 1938

I think it important to emphasize the point that all this is not particularly an *economic* problem, but affects every rational choice concerning conduct where consequences enter into the rational calculation. Generally speaking, in making a decision we have before us a large number of alternatives, none of which is demonstrably more "rational" than the others, in the sense that we can arrange in order of merit the sum aggregate of the benefits obtainable from the complete consequences of each. To avoid being in the position of Buridan's ass, we fall back, therefore, and necessarily do so, on motives of another kind, which are not "rational" in the sense of being concerned with the evaluation of consequences, but are decided by habit, instinct, preference, desire, will, etc. All this is just as true of the non-economic as of the economic man. But it may well be, as you suggest, that when we remember all this, we have to abate somewhat from the traditional picture of the latter.[77]

Thus while the theorist is obliged to tackle the problem using probabilities and equivalent certainties, there is a necessary fuzziness involved in doing so. One is obliged, so to speak, to represent something in a numerical form in one's theory that was not actually a part of the decision process because it was incapable of measurement. Entrepreneurs, for instance, rely on social conventions to form their expectations of quasi rents but the theorist is reduced to tackling their actions analytically in terms of probability. Keynes addressed this point explicitly in 1933 in the lecture (6 November) in which he introduced expected quasi rents.

What degree of precision is advisable in economics? There is the danger of falling into scholasticism, "the essence of which is treating what is vague as what is precise." A generalization to cover everything is impossible and impracticable. Generalizing in economics is thinking by sample, not by generalization. There is no possible use of mechanical logic, you only have it for a sample case not a general

---

76. See my note (Bateman 1992) for a further explication of this argument.
77. *JMK*, xxix, 294.

case. Even mathematical thinking is not in terms of *precise* concepts but "fluffy gray lumps," afterwards you can perhaps discover the *nature* of these "fluffy gray thoughts" although you can never write it down quite precisely (the reason for this is that you are trying to express your theory for those who can't think). There are two reasons for scholasticism: (1) In the early stages of your argument people who disagree raise objections actually because they don't know the score, that is, it is a persuasive expedient; (2) A further reason is that while you may in earlier stages of your work be thinking on the whole correctly, the effort to express it scholastically makes your own fluffiness more real and perhaps may indicate lacunae in your thought.[78]

The inescapable conclusion is that while Keynes was the first economist to construct an interconnected, aggregate model that contained a probabilistic, analytical treatment of economic behavior under uncertainty (albeit a simplistic one), he nonetheless saw this analytical treatment as heuristic and was concerned lest it be reified. The danger with the reification, of course, lay in the possibility that the *real* nature of the decision making process would be lost sight of. For as we will see, once Keynes had achieved this algebra, he no longer possessed a magic formula and the development of good policies required a careful attention to this fact.

Now Patinkin, or anyone else, may impose a modern standard for what constitutes a theory of economic behavior under uncertainty, and Keynes will undoubtedly fail this test. But this kind of retrospective teleology not only obscures the analytical nature of Keynes's treatment, it also hides the fact that he was concerned with reification and (as we shall see) obscures how he changed the basis for his policy recommendations. George Stigler is the most strident proponent of the argument that the theorist's own intentions are unimportant in studying the history of thought, but this argument is fatally flawed for anyone who wishes to preserve the open dialogue necessary for scientific progress.[79] If the only

---

78. From Rymes 1989, 101. Donald Gillies has pointed out to me that the quotation in the second sentence of this quotation is a misquotation of Ramsey (1931, 269) in one of his final essays, "Philosophy." And indeed, much of Keynes's concern in this passage reflects Ramsey's.

79. See Stigler 1965. I have taken special pains in this paragraph to state exactly what I take to be the *sense* of Keynes's use of mathematical expectation in his later work. Recent essays by Carabelli (1991) and O'Donnell (1991) have attributed views to me that do not accurately, or completely, represent my views.

legitimate use of the past is to see how it bears on current theoretical disputes, then the reality of the processes of trial and error that generated progress are to be lost forever. When one reduces the value of the past to the terms of current theoretical dispute, one risks losing a sense of economics as a science. For surely a belief that everything worth knowing is embodied in current theory is an invitation to end the dialogue that defines science. If the history of economic thought is to be useful, it will be in preserving an accurate picture of how progress was achieved in the past.

To see the degree to which Keynes's treatment was novel in its own time, one can consider two cases. One is to consider the treatment of uncertainty in J. R. Hicks's *Value and Capital,* which appeared three years after *The General Theory.* Hicks, who had taught risk at the London School of Economics (LSE) in 1929 and was thus presumably familiar with theories of behavior under uncertainty, nonetheless felt it necessary to introduce the idea of expectations in exactly the same manner Keynes had in his book.[80]

Secondly, and perhaps more importantly, people rarely have *precise* expectations at all. They do not expect that the price at which they will be able to sell a particular output in a particular future week will be just so-and-so much; there will be a certain figure, or range of figures, which they consider most probable, but deviations from this most probable value on either side are considered to be more or less possible. This is a complication which deserves very serious attention.[81]

But while this treatment may seem facile to us, will anyone argue that Hicks was pulling his punches in *Value and Capital?* Summing across the product of each outcome and its probability was still an idea that needed to be introduced explicitly to the reading audience. To judge from this treatment, Keynes's treatment three years earlier was novel stuff indeed to economists.

To further understand the novelty of Keynes's argument one can also note the equivocal nature of Frank Ramsey's own use of mathematical expectation to represent subjective probabilities. Ramsey explicitly denied that the probabilities he was dealing with in his theory were capable of a priori measurement; they were merely something implicit in an agent's actions.

---

80. See Weintraub 1991, 30, for a brief treatment of Hicks's early career at LSE.
81. Hicks 1939, 125.

As soon as we regard belief quantitatively, this seems to me the only view we can take of it. It could well be held that the difference between believing and not believing lies in the presence or absence of introspectible feeling. But when we seek to know what is the difference between believing more firmly and believing less firmly, we can no longer regard it as consisting in having more or less of certain observable feelings; at least I personally cannot recognize any such feelings. The difference seems to me to lie in how far we should act on these beliefs: this may depend on the degree of some feeling or feelings, but I do not know exactly what feelings and I do not see that it is indispensable that we should know. Just the same thing is found in physics; men found that a wire connecting plates of zinc and copper standing in acid deflected a magnetic needle in its neighbourhood. Accordingly as the needle was more or less deflected the wire was said to carry a larger or a smaller current. The nature of this "current" could only be conjectured: what were observed and measured were simply its effects.[82]

According to this theory, probabilities are not necessarily something one consults *before* making one's decisions, but rather something used ex post as measurements of one's willingness to act on one's beliefs (whatever those are). Thus, when Keynes argues that there is no "scientific basis" for forming an expectation of the future and that this causes people to adopt a social convention as the means of forming their expectations, he differs very little from Ramsey; Ramsey's theory does not necessarily presume the existence of anything upon which expectations are based.[83] Likewise, his comments to Bryce and Townshend ("I fancy one has to tackle it on the basis of 'equivalent certainties' ") indicating that a theorist can (or needs to) represent people's actions using probabilities are very much in the spirit of Ramsey's use of mathematical expectation. The *representation* of decisions in this way is merely a pragmatic tool that allows the analyst to treat a decision in a formal way. Keynes was, of course, concerned about the reification of analytical constructs and imbued his warnings about this with great rhetorical flourish; in the end, however, he is the same man we see sending his

---

82. Ramsey 1931, 170.
83. The only substantive difference between Keynes and Ramsey, as Donald Gillies and Grazia Ietto-Gillies (1991) have pointed out, is that Ramsey saw expectations as being formed individually, whereas Keynes saw them as being intersubjective or as being based on group beliefs.

students off into the world with the advice that they must employ these analytical constructs despite the dangers involved in doing so. Ramsey himself approaches the question of the difference between actual human behavior and the representation of it in formal, analytical models from a different direction later in his essay when he discusses induction. The problem he perceives is that while the calculus of probabilities as applied to people's beliefs dictates certain rules for the revision of probabilities when new information is received, people do not actually make these kinds of revisions. There is a "formal logic" (the calculus of probabilities) and a "human logic" (how people actually think): the former can, at best, serve as a guide for testing the consistency of the latter. Ramsey's depiction of "human logic" is particularly interesting, however, from the point of view of Keynes's perception of how people form expectations on the basis of social conventions.

> We have therefore to consider the human mind and what is the most we can ask of it. The human mind works essentially according to general rules or habits; a process of thought not proceeding according to some rule would simply be a random sequence of ideas; whenever we infer *A* from *B* we do so in virtue of some relation between them. We can therefore state the problem of the ideal as "What habits in a general sense would it be best for the human mind to have?"[84]

What indeed are social conventions if not "general rules or habits"?

Thus, seen in the fuller context of his times, it seems reasonable to believe that Keynes's treatment of uncertainty was indeed a pathbreaking effort to introduce new ideas to economics. The introduction of confidence, per se, to monetary theory was not a revolution; Marshall had borrowed an idea that was already quite old when he made confidence a part of the Cambridge explanation of the trade cycle. What was revolutionary in Keynes's treatment was a model to explicitly analyze how confidence worked in the economy; this meant building the model of effective demand and introducing an analytical treatment of expectations into it. There is no way to separate the development of his model of effective demand from Keynes's concerns with uncertainty. Uncertainty reentered Keynes's thought after his attempt to sever himself from the Cambridge confidence tradition in the *Treatise* left him unable to explain the financial upheaval in the early 1930s. As uncertainty reentered his

---

84. Ramsey 1931, 194.

thought, it provided him with the element he needed to "link one thing together with another" and thus served as the cement for his "monetary theory of production." The nature of his analytical treatment of uncertainty is a virtual mirror image of Ramsey's treatment— probabilities are merely a *representation* of deeply held beliefs that may not have been formed with any conscious attention to these "implicit" probabilities. And while it is true that this treatment is a far cry from modern treatments of uncertainty, it was a pathbreaking treatment in its own time.

Part 4
Conclusion

CHAPTER 6

Keynes's Uncertain Revolution

The reason we still know Keynes's name is undoubtedly its connection with the question of the appropriate role for the state in a capitalist economy. There are many other intriguing aspects of his life that help to make him a notable figure—his connection to Bloomsbury, his marriage to Lydia Lopokova, his role in the Apostles—but it is the *Keynesian Revolution* in economic policy that keeps him on center stage. One need only consider the fate of Alfred Marshall's reputation to see the point; while Marshall is one of the few modern economists of equal stature with Keynes, it seems safe to say that he has no *public* identity today. One would never find Marshall's name, for instance, as a code word in an editorial, or leader.

Keynes, however, has an instantly recognizable name. As the father of the Keynesian Revolution, we know him as the man who provided the theoretical foundations for government intervention in the economy when the Western world was paralyzed by the Great Depression. When capitalism appeared on its last legs, Keynes is the man who came to its rescue with his ideas about how the government could undertake large budget deficits and public works projects to lift the economy into recovery.

For nearly 25 years, historians have been trying to debunk the mythical elements in this picture but with no effect on Keynes's reputation. We know now, for instance, that the arguments among economists for large-scale public works projects during the Great Depression came from all ideological quarters and predated the publication of *The General Theory*.[1] We also know that economic management by the state proceeded in most nations along trajectories that have little to do with Keynes or his great book. Interestingly, however, the excellent collection of essays that has most forcefully brought home this last point, *The*

---

1. T. W. Hutchison (1953, 1968) and J. Ronnie Davis (1971) have pointed out the widespread advocacy of public works projects and budget deficits *before* the publication of *The General Theory*.

Political Power of Economic Ideas, is subtitled *Keynesianism Across Nations.*[2] Thus, despite our growing understanding that Keynes and his work are generally not directly involved in the rise of economic management by the state, we still label this phenomenon *Keynesianism.*

This willingness to attach Keynes's name to a large-scale historical phenomenon in which he (and his ideas) played little direct role seems motivated by two influences. One is simply inertial; we have thought of this process as "Keynesianism" for so long, and the phrase has such an obvious meaning, that we are not inclined to change our usage. This is just as in the case of our use of the term Marxist to describe the economic systems in the formerly totalitarian states in Eastern Europe; although these systems were not run on any principles attributable to Marx himself, we call them Marxist because the term is convenient and has a familiar meaning for us.[3] The second reason that we are willing to use Keynes's name as a label for economic management by the state is in recognition of his unique achievement in *The General Theory.* Even if he and his ideas cannot be *directly* implicated in the rise of state management in most nations, he is seen as the first one to cross the finish line in the race to provide a sound theoretical basis for such intervention.

In one sense, the story of Keynes's theoretical triumph is undoubtedly true. The model at the heart of *The General Theory* is the first model to successfully show how employment is affected by aggregate demand in a capitalist economy. Although it has been shown that many parts of Keynes's model were anticipated by others, no one anticipated his *whole* model of how the aggregate level of demand in the economy determines the overall level of employment.[4] And it was exactly this model that was first required in order to make a *theoretical* argument about how the government could successfully intervene to raise the level of employment; people may have had clear ideas about how to spur the economy, but they had no fully articulated model to show how their programs would work before the publication of *The General Theory.*

Oddly, however, Keynes spends little time in the book discussing the fiscal policies that might follow from his model. After completing his

---

2. It is in no way the intention of the contributors to this volume to "debunk" Keynes. Rather, in the process of trying to examine the actual processes by which demand management policies were instituted, they have discovered in most cases that the policies that were later to be identified as Keynesian had good currency before they obtained Keynes's imprimatur. These ideas are often labeled "Proto-Keynesian" in this volume.

3. There is also the fact, of course, that the Eastern Europeans promulgated the idea that their economic policies were somehow derived from Marx's teachings.

4. Patinkin 1982 has provided the definitive study in this regard.

model, he uses it to animate a theory of the trade cycle, but one searches in vain for a clear-cut argument for the kind of activist, short-run policies associated with his name. Why did Keynes pull up short of a full-fledged argument for "Keynesian" policies? One explanation is to rely on Keynes's claim in the book's preface that his intention was largely theoretical: "This book is chiefly addressed to my fellow economists. I hope that it will be intelligible to others. But its main purpose is to deal with difficult questions of theory, and only in the second place with the application of this theory to practice."[5] Trying to limit Keynes's intention to theory development, however, ignores the conclusion of this statement and his express concern with "the application of this theory to practice." The question thus remains why it is that the "application to practice" is largely in terms of articulating a theory of the trade cycle, rather than to advocating activist fiscal policy.

The answer to the mystery of Keynes's reticence seems to lie in his growing concern with confidence. The very element that served to "link one thing together with another" and pushed him over the theoretical threshold to *The General Theory* also helped to temper his arguments in favor of activist policy. Earlier in the decade, when he had been forced to face up to the importance of confidence in financial markets, he had deftly sidestepped the more conservative policy arguments of those like Hubert Henderson who were already committed to the importance of confidence in the Slump. Indeed, 18 months after the dégringolade that accompanied the abandonment of the gold standard, Keynes was to make his impassioned call for activist fiscal policy in *The Means to Prosperity*. But in the months and years that followed, as he honed his newfound faith in the importance of confidence, he came to occupy a much less strident position on public works and activist policy.[6]

In *The General Theory* itself, Keynes's real focus as regards the stabilization of the economy is on monetary policy and on a vague and ambiguous concept that he labels "the socialization of investment." This term includes many different things in Keynes's argument; the capital development plans of the utility companies, the building plans of local authorities, the encouragement (and discouragement) of new housing construction, and, not least, the maintenance of the expectations of the

---

5. Keynes 1936, v.

6. The change in the general tone of Keynes's arguments and their distance from the traditional Keynesian position is captured nicely in the last chapter of Clarke 1988. See also Colander 1984.

capitalist class. Some of this, of course, does involve fiscal policy, but "the socialization of investment" cannot properly be taken as a synonym for "fiscal policy."[7] The term is, rather, a catchall phrase that reflects Keynes's growing awareness that economic management is not a simple mechanistic task; while he never gave up his hope that something could be done, he was, after finishing *The General Theory,* less sure of exactly what that something was and how it might be achieved. The magic formula mentality that he had employed in constructing *A Treatise on Money* disappeared once confidence moved to the center of his analytical concerns.

Thus, both the *Keynesian* Revolution and *Keynes's* Revolution are of a different nature than that we normally ascribe to them.[8] As regards the expanding role of the state in the management of the economy, we now know that this is a much more complex story than the world suddenly embracing Keynes's "new" ideas. As regards Keynes himself, it is misleading to suggest that his concern with fiscal policy was unchanged and unabated after the publication of *Can Lloyd George Do It?* in 1929. Likewise, it is misleading to suggest that *The General Theory* is a fully worked out theoretical underpinning for the proposals he made in 1933 in *The Means to Prosperity.* Keynes never abandoned a belief that public works projects might have some value in stabilizing the economy, but he saw them after 1936 as having a limited role. The conclusion of this story, then, is how Keynes came to recognize that there were *limits* to the state's ability to manage the economy.

"The Socialization of Investment"

As Alan Meltzer has pointed out, first-time readers of *The General Theory* are often struck by what is *not* in the book; most notably the lack of any strong argument in favor of activist fiscal policy.[9] For economists trained in the decades after the Second World War, the book's approach to monetary policy is also discombobulating. Raised to believe that Keynes had come to the position that "money doesn't matter" (i.e., that monetary policy is unimportant), it is odd to find that this is not his

---

7. Patinkin (1982, 200–14; 1983, 49) argues not that the two terms are synonymous, but that public works projects were a large and important part of the socialization of investment. A careful reading of Keynes's texts, however, shows that one is ignoring much of Keynes's argument if one tries to conflate the two.

8. Clarke (1990, 206) has nicely described the problems inherent in trying to paint a "unilinear" picture of the Keynesian Revolution.

9. See Meltzer 1981, 1988.

position at all. For while he argues that monetary policy alone cannot raise an economy out of a slump, he actually has a well-articulated stance as to the difference between good and bad monetary policy and a clear belief that good (stable) monetary policy is a necessary part of a well-functioning capitalist economy.[10]

Taken together, this asymmetrical treatment of fiscal and monetary policy is further disconcerting in that the explicit treatment of monetary policy belies the argument (mentioned previously) that the book was only meant as a theoretical tract. Granted that theoretical innovation was one of the book's primary purposes, it is impossible to argue that Keynes did not also mean to have the theory applied to policy problems, given his argument for the importance of a stable policy of keeping long-run interest rates as low as possible.

Don Patinkin has tried to defend the more traditional interpretation of *The General Theory* as a book meant to promote activist fiscal policy by arguing that Keynes's frequent references to "the socialization of investment" are in many cases references to public works projects.[11] According to this interpretation, these many references are calls for the activist policy that follows from Keynes's revolutionary new model. The large number of actions that Keynes subsumed under this rubric, however, taken together with the limitations he acknowledged to large-scale public work projects, make Patinkin's interpretation questionable. In addition, one would expect that a person who had made a highly successful journalistic career by articulating the position for activist policies would have had no problem in making a similar argument in an academic tract (as is borne out by his arguments in *The General Theory* for a stable long-run policy of low interest rates). If Keynes had meant "the socialization of investment" as an analogue for "undertaking public works projects" it seems that he could, and would, have said exactly that.

There is, thus, more to Keynes's concept of the socialization of investment than debt-financed public works; seen in historical context, the idea has much broader implications than this traditional interpretation suggests. Following his acceptance of the position that confidence is an important element in the success of government policies, Keynes once again became an advocate of the idea that the business cycle is the result of oscillations in business confidence. "I suggest that the essential character of the Trade Cycle and, especially, the regularity of time-

---

10. See Moggridge and Howson 1974; Meltzer 1981, 1988; and Bateman 1991a.
11. See note 7.

sequence and of duration which justifies us in calling it a *cycle,* is mainly
due to the way in which the marginal efficiency of capital fluctuates." It
was this position, that *stabilizing business confidence* would be necessary
to mitigate the business cycle, that undergirded his concept of the socialization of investment.

The connection between the trade cycle and the socialization of
investment is first made clear in chapter 22 of *The General Theory,*
Keynes's "Notes on the Trade Cycle."[12]

> Thus with markets organized and influenced as they are at present,
> the market estimation of the marginal efficiency of capital may
> suffer such enormously wide fluctuations that it cannot be suffi-
> ciently offset by corresponding fluctuations in the rate of interest.
> Moreover, the corresponding movements in the stock-market may,
> as we have seen above, depress the propensity to consume just
> when it is most needed. In conditions of *laissez-faire* the avoidance
> of wide fluctuations in employment may, therefore, prove impossi-
> ble without a far-reaching change in the psychology of investment
> markets such as there is no reason to expect. I conclude that the
> duty of ordering the current volume of investment cannot safely be
> left in private hands.[13]

But as Keynes makes clear in his concluding chapter, he does not mean
nationalization or state control of industry when he refers to the socialization of investment.

> In some other respects the foregoing theory is moderately conser-
> vative in its implications. For whilst it indicates the vital impor-
> tance of establishing certain central controls in matters which are
> now left in the main to individual initiative, there are wide fields
> of activity which are unaffected. The State will have to exercise a
> guiding influence on the propensity to consume partly through its
> scheme of taxation, partly by fixing the rate of interest, and partly,

---

12. Patinkin (1983, 48–49; 1990, 226–27) argues that this chapter is not integral to
The General Theory because it comes in the last section of the book, entitled "Short Notes
Suggested by the General Theory." For several reasons, I take this to be an unfortunate
strategy in historical interpretation, not least because it seems an attempt to edit Keynes's
work for him. Because the chapter fits well with the rest of Keynes's book and in the
historical context of the evolution of his thought, it seems an important part of explaining
what Keynes was thinking when he published the book.

13. Keynes 1936, 320–21.

perhaps, in other ways. Furthermore, it seems unlikely that the influence of banking policy on the rate of interest will be sufficient by itself to determine an optimum rate of investment. I conceive, therefore, that a somewhat comprehensive socialization of investment will prove the only means of securing an approximation to full employment; though this need not exclude all manner of compromises and of devices by which public authority will cooperate with private initiative. But beyond this no obvious case is made out for a system of State Socialism which would embrace most of the economic life of the community. It is not the ownership of the instruments of production which it is important for the State to assume. If the State is able to determine the aggregate amount of resources devoted to augmenting the instruments and the basic rate of reward to those who own them, it will have accomplished all that is necessary. Moreover, the necessary measures of socialization can be introduced gradually and without a break in the general traditions of society.[14]

Taken together, these two statements demonstrate the apparent ambiguity in Keynes's proposal. On the one hand, the problem of "the psychology of the investment market" is so deep and intransigent in a laissez-faire economy that "ordering the current volume of investment cannot safely be left in private hands." On the other hand, he in no way intends for the state to take ownership or control of capital out of the private sector. What then does he intend? Just what is the "socialization of investment"?

There is clear evidence in the text that Keynes did not mean the simple substitution of public works projects for private investment. This answer would, of course, offer a way out of the apparent dilemma of leaving capital in private hands while at the same time arguing that the investment that results when private investors are left to their own devices is insufficient to maintain full employment; investment by the state could replace investment in the private sector. But by this time, Keynes was unable to see things in such a mechanical light. Because the trade cycle was driven by expectations, it was impossible to ignore the effect of policy on businessmen's outlooks.

This (the fact that the trade cycle is driven by expectations) means, unfortunately, not only that slumps and depressions are exagger-

---

14. Ibid., 377–78.

ated in degree, but that economic prosperity is excessively dependent on a political and social atmosphere which is congenial to the
average business man. If the fear of a Labour Government or a New
Deal depresses enterprise, this need not be the result either of a
reasonable calculation or of a plot with political intent;—it is the
mere consequence of upsetting the delicate balance of spontaneous
optimism. In estimating the prospects of investment, we must have
regard, therefore, to the nerves and hysteria and even the diges-
tions and reactions to the weather of those upon whose spontaneous
activity it largely depends.[15]

Keynes was now keenly aware of the possibility that public works might
displace private investment and so whatever he meant by "the socialization of investment," it was more than the simple use of public works
projects as a makeweight for private investment. His many years of
work in economic policy making had finally caused a change in his
perspective on this question.

"A Conventional Approach to Policy"

Thus, by the time Keynes had gotten to *The General Theory* he had a
much more complex idea of what a good policy would be than he had
had in the period 1929–33 when he had advocated large-scale, loan-
financed government work schemes. In the earlier period, he had dismissed the importance of confidence in the recovery, saying that it
would return *after* the programs he proposed had worked to stimulate
profits and employment. Now he was ready to admit that a lack of
confidence could scotch even a program undertaken with the best of
intentions.

But what, then, would constitute a good, effective policy to keep
the economy at full employment? If it was not possible to simply adjust
the volume of loan expenditure, then what *could* be done?

It helps, perhaps, in trying to answer these questions, to look first at
Keynes's proposals for monetary policy. His ideas here are straightforward and reveal a clear understanding of the problems posed by confidence and uncertainty. The key to Keynes's ideas about monetary policy
was his new concept of liquidity preference; the amount of cash that
people choose to hold is the crucial element in determining the rate of
interest. When the demand for cash balances is high, ceteris paribus,

---

15. Ibid., 162.

interest rates will be, too, since the public's efforts to increase their cash holdings will cause interest rates to rise. Conversely, when the demand for cash balances is low, interest rates will be low.

Unfortunately, this means changes in liquidity preference may undercut efforts by the monetary authorities to stimulate the economy. If the central bank's actions cause changes in the public's desire to hold cash, then their efforts may be self-defeating. "Changes in the liquidity function itself, due to a change in the news which causes revision of expectations, will often be discontinuous, and will, therefore, give rise to a corresponding discontinuity of change in the rate of interest."[16] Should the authorities, for instance, try to increase the amount of money in circulation in hopes that its ready availability will cause interest rates to *fall,* the policy might backfire because the public's demand to hold cash will increase so much that interest rates will actually *rise.*

It might be more accurate, perhaps, to say that the rate of interest is a highly conventional rather than a highly psychological, phenomenon. For its actual value is largely governed by the prevailing view as to what its value is expected to be. *Any* level of interest which is accepted with sufficient conviction as *likely* to be durable *will* be durable; subject, of course, in a changing society to fluctuations for all kinds of reasons round the expected normal. In particular, when M_1 is increasing faster than M, the rate of interest will rise, and *vice versa.* But it may fluctuate for decades about a level which is chronically too high for full employment.[17]

The conundrum for the monetary authorities thus lies in fluctuating expectations. Fortunately, however, most people form their expectations according to what they take to be the "conventional" view of the effects of policy. This means that if the authorities can foster a belief in their intention to keep interest rates low, the public's belief in this policy will be self-fulfilling; if the policy *convention* is one of keeping long-term interest rates low, then a *conventional outlook* will form among the public that this will be the case. One good convention leads to another.[18]

This answers, in part, the question of "What would constitute a good, effective policy to keep the economy at full employment?" As regards monetary policy, the answer is a (stable) policy of low long-term

16. Ibid., 198.
17. Ibid., 203–4 (italics in original).
18. This argument adumbrates a part of Bateman 1991a.

interest rates. Just as importantly, it points to the answer to the second question, "If it is not possible to simply adjust the volume of loan-expenditure, then what *can* be done?" As Keynes's vision of the possibilities for economic policy changed and matured after 1933, he came to see that maintaining the proper conventions was crucial to investment, too. Just as a well-established convention of low interest rates might be self-fulfilling, so, too, might be a well-established convention of stable, high levels of investment.

The essence, however, of this "socialization of investment" was more complex than in the case of monetary policy; decisions to make expenditures on capital outlay were vested in many places, rather than in one central authority, so there was no analogue to the central bank. One agency could not simply make a decision, as with monetary policy, which then only needed to be accepted (with confidence) by the public. Whereas in the case of monetary policy the public could be induced to hold (financial) assets by the reassurance that the authorities would keep their future yields at an appropriate level, in the case of investment in plant and equipment the future yield on these (physical) assets would be determined by many factors. Thus, the socialization of investment would necessarily involve something more than was involved with monetary policy; many kinds of good conventions would be necessary to obtain the high (and stable) levels of investment necessary to maintain full employment.[19]

The three most prominent ways in which Keynes meant to socialize investment by creating new conventions were revealed in the years following the publication of *The General Theory*. Keynes did not ever actually use his ambiguous phrase again, but it is clear in his writings from 1937 to 1946 that he was trying to find practical manifestations for the ideas that flowed from his book, and in particular, how effective demand could be stabilized by the stabilization of investment. In both his public writings (essays, articles, and letters to the editor) and his policy work (Commodity Policy, the Beveridge Plan, the White Paper on *Employment Policy*, and the National Debt Enquiry), he developed various arguments and proposals aimed at stabilizing the aggregate level of

---

19. The importance of conventions to Keynes's arguments in *The General Theory* is now widely recognized. See, for instance, Runde 1991 and Littleboy 1990. The works that are perhaps most responsible for this turn in Keynesian interpretation are Tony Lawson's (1985) widely cited essay and Anna Carabelli's (1988) book. My interpretation differs from any in this body of literature, both for bringing Keynes to this position through a different historical sequence and for containing a different argument as regards Keynes's attitude toward the possibilities and usefulness of economic analysis.

investment. Not surprisingly, given the importance that he attached to expectations in his theory of investment, the three means to stabilization were closely interconnected.

Socializing Public Investment

One way in which Keynes hoped to socialize investment was through what he called the Public Corporations. He argued that two-thirds to three-fourths of Britain's capital stock was under the control of "corporations" that were regulated by the state or served a public function. He included the utilities, the port and dock authorities, the London County Council, and building contractors in this category. This part of the capital stock, which "lie(s) half way between private and public control," seemed an obvious point of departure for developing a new convention. Keynes had written in the 1920s about the importance of the distinction between private and public corporations, especially during the Liberal Industrial Inquiry, but had dropped such talk from his policy repertoire with the publication of the *Treatise*. There are, however, important differences between his vision of the 1920s and his vision after 1936.

One difference is between the *purposes* of his argument in the two periods. In the 1920s he had tried to argue that there were insufficient grounds for nationalizing large-scale industry. After *The General Theory*, on the other hand, he tried to argue that these large-scale industries could be relied upon for increasing and decreasing investment as was necessary for the society as a whole. These two arguments might not necessarily be so different, of course, if one just takes them to be two cases of arguing that public managers can be expected to do the "right" thing, but there is more than this to the difference.

In arguing against nationalization in the 1920s, Keynes was trying to make a point about the day-to-day operation of the public corporations. The issues at stake involved whether or not the corporations worked for the public good (rather than the stockholders' good) and whether they were managed efficiently. He argued that these corporations already attempted both to please their customers and to avoid public controversy because of their high public profile; thus, provided that more information was made public regarding their accounts, Keynes believed that adequate pressure would exist to insure that the public interest was served. Likewise, he argued that it would be possible to recruit top-notch managers to run the existing public corporations without nationalizing them.

His argument after *The General Theory* was quite different. Now instead of arguing that good men in the right position will do the right thing, Keynes argued that the control of investment by the public corporations should take place through the auspices of a "board of public investment." This board would encourage the public corporations to prepare "detailed plans" of the projects that they could profitably undertake. The board would then make financial (and design) critiques of these plans and give them back to the managers for reworking. In this way, "some large and useful projects, at least, can be launched at a few months' notice."[20]

In stark contrast to his advice in the 1920s, however, Keynes understood the last step in this process of controlling public investment to lie *outside* the corporations.[21] Rather than relying on an argument that the managers of the public corporations would undertake particular projects just when the nation needed them to, he vested the responsibility for initiating the projects with the *monetary authorities*.

There can be no justification for a rate of interest which impedes an adequate flow of new projects at a time when the national resources for production are not fully employed. The rate of interest must be reduced to the figure that the new projects can afford. In special cases subsidies may be justified; but in general it is the long-term rate of interest which should come down to the figure which the marginal project can earn. We have the power to achieve this. The Bank of England and the Treasury had a great success at the time of the conversion of the War Loan. But it is possible that they still underrate the extent of their powers. With the existing control over the exchanges which has revolutionized the technical position, and with the vast resources at the disposal of the authorities through the Bank of England, the Exchange Equalization Fund, and other funds under the control of the Treasury, it lies within their power, by the exercise of the moderation, the gradualness, and the discreet handling of the market of which they have shown themselves to be masters, to make the long-term rate of interest what they choose within reason. If we know what rate of interest is required to make profitable a flow of new projects at the proper pace, we have the power to make that rate prevail in the market.[22]

Keynes had suggested that the investment board should see that the public corporations rank their projects according to the interest rate that

---

20. Keynes 1937, 394.
21. Skidelsky's (1989) argument that Keynes's writings about "socialized firms" are consistent throughout the 1920s and 1930s is clearly mistaken.
22. *JMK*, xxi, 395.

would make them profitable; it would then be the responsibility of the Bank of England and the Treasury to take the next step and trigger the projects ("at a few months' notice") by lowering interest rates. This change in Keynes's approach to the public corporations may have been due to many causes. He may, for instance, have dropped his belief that good managers were likely to seek employment with such concerns. Or he may have ceased believing in the likelihood that any manager in such a position, left to his own, was likely to include the national interest in his firm's investment plans. The most likely reason, however, was the argument that he had first encountered in the Macmillan Committee that the planning horizon for new investment was too long to make countercyclical policy feasible. These objections from the Treasury had focused on public works projects, but Keynes almost certainly came to see their general point after so many years of hearing the argument. In order to provide an adequate flow of investment, the government's projects would have to be planned well ahead.

Public Works and a Balanced Budget

Just as Keynes's approach to the management of public investment changed over time, so too did his approach to public works projects. Whereas in 1929 and 1933 he had argued for discretionary, large-scale projects to address problems in the short run, by 1944 he was arguing for a regularly planned program of government capital expenditure. Seen in historical context, as part of the evolution of his thinking, this change seems to have been motivated by his concern with business confidence.

His concern with confidence, however, was not solely about how businessmen viewed the budgetary situation. While he continued to be worried about this and recognized the potential for "upsetting the delicate balance of spontaneous optimism,"[23] he was also worried about the problem of setting up mistaken expectations of a rapid expansion with poorly timed projects. This is most obvious in his collection of three short essays that appeared in *The Times* in January 1937. At this time, less than a year after the publication of *The General Theory,* Britain was experiencing a pickup in economic activity and Keynes was interested in how to sustain it. But with unemployment hovering between 10 and 11 percent, we find Keynes in the surprising position of arguing *against* any further stimulus from public works.

---

23. Keynes 1936, 162.

Part of Keynes's reluctance to increase loan expenditure was his belief that current expenditures could be better directed. He believed that refocusing the *direction* of current spending would yield important results that an outright increase in expenditure would not. "We are in more need of a rightly distributed demand than of a greater aggregate demand; and the Treasury would be entitled to economize elsewhere to compensate for the cost of special assistance to the distressed areas."

The real crux of his argument, however, was that continued loan expenditure at the time was likely to cause overexpansion through a sequence of mistaken expectations.

The longer the recovery has lasted, the more difficult does it become to maintain the stability of new investment. Some of the investment which properly occurs during a recovery is, in the nature of things, nonrecurrent; for example, the increase in working capital as output increases and the provision of additional equipment to keep pace with the improvement in consumption. Another part becomes less easy to sustain, not because saturation point has been reached, but because with each increase in our stock of wealth the profit to be expected from a further increase declines. And, thirdly, the abnormal profits obtainable, during a too rapid recovery of demand, from equipment which is temporarily in short supply is likely to lead to exaggerated expectations from certain types of new investment, the disappointment of which will bring a subsequent reaction. Experience shows that this is sure to occur if aggregate investment is allowed to rise for a time above the normal proper proportion. We can also add that the rise in stock exchange values consequent on the recovery usually leads to a certain amount of expenditure paid for, not out of current income, but out of stock exchange profits, which will cease when values cease to rise further. It is evident, therefore, what a ticklish business it is to maintain stability. We have to be preparing the way for an increase in sound investments of the second type which have not yet reached saturation point, to take the place in due course of the investment of the first type which is necessarily noncurrent, while at the same time avoiding a temporary overlap of investments of the first and second types liable to increase aggregate investment to an excessive figure, which by inflating profits will induce unsound investment of the third type based on mistaken expectations.[24]

---

24. *JMK*, xxi, 387–88.

Thus, the state faced two problems in the use of public works: killing spontaneous optimism and creating too much of it. The right way to avoid a slump was to create a slow path to a higher level of aggregate investment. This concern was still evident a year later when, after the slump he feared had come, Keynes found himself arguing about the proper role of public works projects in stimulating recovery.

Public loan expenditure is not, of course the only way, and not necessarily the best way, to increase employment. Nor is it always sufficiently effective to overcome other adverse influences. The state of confidence and of expectation about what will happen next, the conditions of credit, the rate of interest, the growth of population, the state of foreign trade, and the readiness of the public to spend are scarcely less important.[25]

Keynes clearly saw the proper use of public works as determined, in part, by its effect on private investment, instability in the one-quarter to one-third of new investment that lay in private hands possibly being enough to offset the effects of any government program.

But despite their consistent focus on expectations, Keynes's statements in 1937–38 are of an unsystematic nature. His heart attack in March 1937 kept him from his usual busy schedule and he made no attempt in the years following the publication of *The General Theory* to lay out his general conception of economic policy making. Economic circumstances, too, undoubtedly kept him from focusing on the "normal" policy making, as rearmament and war planning were about to take center stage.

The only really systematic statement of his views after *The General Theory* comes from his pamphlet, *How to Pay for the War* (1940) and in his work on postwar planning between 1942 and 1945. Of these, it is his work on postwar policy that provides the clearest insights into his thinking on public works. In 1942, and again in 1945, Keynes advocated that the budget be broken down into two parts, the Exchequer's Budget (ordinary government expenditure) and a Public Capital Budget (which would include loan-financed public works).[26] He argued strongly that the government should always plan to balance the Exchequer's budget. "It is important to emphasize that it is no part of the

---

25. Ibid., xxi, 429–30.
26. These were actually old ideas for Keynes. He was responsible for the part of the Liberal Industrial Inquiry (1928) that advocated separating the budget into two parts.

purpose of the Exchequer or the Public Capital Budget to facilitate deficit financing, as I understand this term."[27] In fact, he argued that the Exchequer's budget could best be kept in balance by such a scheme as he advocated; if public capital expenditure was successfully undertaken on a regular, planned basis so as to help dampen the trade cycle through the creation of an expectation of more stable aggregate demand, then receipts and expenditures in the Exchequer's budget would be stabilized and so make it less likely that it would ever become unbalanced in the first place.

This focus on a balanced Exchequer's budget differentiates Keynes from traditional Keynesians in two senses. The first is his obvious emphasis on balanced budgets as against the normal type of Keynesian argument that unbalanced ordinary budgets can be used as a countercyclical tool.[28] The second, related difference is his belief that consumption would make a poor countercyclical policy tool; the typical Keynesian argument that a deficit, regardless of how incurred, will be stimulatory depends on the premise that the changes in tax receipts will cause changes in consumption. This second difference is clear in his arguments as early as 1943, and he stressed it in correspondence with James Meade, one of the young economists in the Economic Section of the War Cabinet who was more inclined at the time to activist policies.

I have much less confidence than you have in off-setting proposals which aim at short-period changes in consumption. I agree with Henderson that one has to pay great attention to securing the right long-period trend in the propensity to consume. But the amount one can do in the short period is likely to be meagre. I think it may

---

27. *JMK*, xxvii, 406; see also 352–53.

28. Patinkin (1990, 225–33) has focused on Keynes's willingness to use the public capital budget as a countercyclical tool as evidence of an unchanged interest on his part in activist fiscal policy. This would seem an inappropriate inference, however, given his many earlier (1937–38) statements concerning the expectational effects of such policies and the toned down, guarded nature of his comments in his last years. While Keynes *did* allow that once a successful program of regular public capital expenditure was begun it might eventually be possible to speed up or slow down some part of this program to offset fluctuations in private investment, he steadfastly maintained that the primary purpose of the public capital budget was to establish a stable long-run program that would in turn lead to the expectation of more stability. It is also worth noting that Keynes believed that there would have to be considerably more information available than was currently the case before the authorities would have the kind of data necessary to know about impending changes in private investment. See especially *JMK*, xxvii, 368–69.

be a tactical error to stress so much an unorthodox method, very difficult to put over, if, in addition to its unpopularity, it is not very likely to be efficacious.[29]

The more fully formed picture that emerges from this systematic treatment during the war is one of public works as a *preventative* tool rather than something that can regularly be used as a short-term, discretionary policy tool. Used properly, Keynes seems to argue, they can help to alleviate the problems with expectations in both phases of the cycle. These might be occasions to speed up, or slow down, expenditure on capital projects, but these would be *preventative* steps and involve changes in a well-planned, preexisting agenda. During the downturn, there need be no fear of a large-scale project that would lead to budgetary problems; on the upswing, there was no need to overstimulate expectations with unnecessary and poorly timed projects. Thus, the judicious use of public capital expenditure could be made a new convention that would yield more stability in the level of aggregate investment.

Stabilizing Private Investment

Keynes was never explicit about exactly what steps the government might take to insure the stability of private investment. That is, he never advocated a formal mechanism by which the volume of private investment could be adjusted to a particular level. The reason is not far to seek.

In *The General Theory,* Keynes had lain particular stress on the role of expectations in determining the amount of private investment and had attributed the trade cycle to the fluctuations in aggregate investment caused by changes in the expectations of investors. The key, then, to "controlling" private investment was to stabilize the "uncontrollable and disobedient psychology of the business world." No mechanical formula or easy state directive could accomplish this task, and Keynes had no illusion that he could offer one.

Instead he offered his proposals for stable monetary policy and the socialization of *public* investment with the intention that both would help to create more stable expectations among *private* investors. It is difficult to know, perhaps, what order of magnitude he placed on the relative importance of private investment, given his idea that it constituted only a quarter to a third of total investment,

---

29. *JMK,* xxvii, 326.

but it was clearly enough that he was willing to acknowledge that the adverse effect on business confidence of ill-conceived public projects could undermine the state's efforts to stabilize the economy. Thus, private investment still had an important role to play in stabilizing a capitalist economy.

It took several more years, however, after the publication of *The General Theory,* to work out all the dimensions of his plan. Although he had a good idea in 1937 of how a national board of investment, together with the central bank, might influence the rate of investment of the public corporations, it was not until he began work on postwar planning that he glimpsed the full possibility of using public works expenditure to help maintain a balanced budget.[30] With the ordinary budget in balance, and with public works financed separately as self-liquidating projects, the type of shocks to confidence of which Henderson had so often complained should no longer be a problem. The construction and maintenance of the necessary infrastructure could be made a regular part of the state's work in such a way that it lent to the stability of employment.

Once he had developed his ideas for establishing new conventions to use monetary policy, the public corporations, and public works to stabilize aggregate investment, his hope was that an expectation would form that full employment could and would be maintained. For instance, in his comments on the various documents that led up to the publication of the White Paper on *Employment Policy,* he emphasized the importance of the *prevention* of cycles through the careful use of public investment, rather than short-period, discretionary efforts at countercyclical expenditure. And as the White Paper neared completion, his comments often turned to the overall effect of a full-employment policy on confidence.

> Such a procedure as this might give greatly increased confidence to the public that the maintenance of employment and national income was now an avowed and deliberate aim of financial and economic policy."[31]

> I believe that the announcement by the Chancellor of a presentation on the above lines would have an enormous public success, since it would greatly increase confidence that the Full Employment policy is intended seriously.[32]

---

30. The best survey of Keynes's thinking on budgetary policy is in Dimsdale 1987.
31. *JMK,* xxvii, 369.
32. *JMK,* xxvii, 413.

If a conventional outlook could be established that the economy would run at full tilt, then his new policy conventions would be successful.

"Rules and Conventions Skillfully Put across and Guilefully Preserved"

From the perspective of the late twentieth century, it is ironic that Maynard Keynes ended his career as the proponent of several "policy rules" that he believed could help to mitigate the trade cycle. The irony stems from the fact that macroeconomists today tend to advocate one of two mutually exclusive approaches to stabilization: a person is either in favor of rules (e.g., constant money growth and a balanced budget) or of discretionary countercyclical policies (e.g., fluctuating interest rates and cyclically unbalanced budgets). But while those who advocate rules come in many varieties (monetarists, rational expectationists, new classicals, and constitutional economists), those who advocate discretionary policies are invariably labeled as *Keynesians*.

Keynes's specific proposals do not fit well into either camp.[33] Those who want a rules-based monetary policy believe in a money growth rule rather than an interest rate target; the experience of the great inflation in the 1970s has disabused everyone of the idea that the central bank can easily maintain a policy of low long-term interest rates while still keeping prices in check. And few, if any, of the economists interested in balanced budgets see public works (and a separate capital budget) as the appropriate means of achieving their desideratum. Likewise, no school of thought comes readily to mind as the proponents of a national investment board to help lay the groundwork for the capital planning of public corporations; in fact, the recent widespread push for privatization from both the left and the right, taken together with the "restructuring" of private capital in the last decade, seems to make the public corporation an antiquated idea.

The fact remains, however, that Keynes advocated stable policy conventions and that he did so for the same reasons that many contemporary theorists do so; he realized that the use of short-term, discretionary policies as a reaction to the trade cycle was likely to set up adverse expectations that blunted their effectiveness. Repeatedly, after 1936, he backed away from the kind of grandiose policies he had advocated earlier in his life. Repeatedly he argued against the types of policies that

---

33. Patinkin (1990, 225–33) has offered the most trenchant critique of attempts to fit Keynes into the more modern camp of rules advocates.

we identify today as Keynesian. Keynes, after *The General Theory,* believed that stable, long-run policies were the best route to successfully stabilizing the economy.[34]

There is another fine irony, of course, in Keynes becoming an advocate of the use of rules and conventions to help create a better world. Whereas as a young man he had devoted himself to the study of probability in order to disprove G. E. Moore's argument for the importance of established rules and conventions, he now found himself as an old man arguing in favor of rules and conventions as the necessary means to maintaining liberal civilization. As a young man he had constructed an objective theory of probability to help establish the individual's right to ignore society's rules and make an independent judgment of the right course of action; as an old man he found it necessary to argue in favor of rules because of the "uncontrollable and disobedient" psychology of businessmen. Objective probabilities had made it possible to *ignore rules;* intersubjective probabilities made it necessary to *follow rules.*

Keynes himself was aware of the change in his outlook. In "My Early Beliefs" he reported, "We were not aware that civilization was a thin and precarious crust erected by the personality and the will of a very few, and only maintained by rules and conventions skillfully put across and guilefully preserved." The change was not a bitter pill, however, for he was now able to see the sorts of rules he was advocating as the means to a good life. He explicitly endorsed Moore's "fundamental intuitions" in "My Early Beliefs," saying only that Moore's menu of the ideal— friendship, love, and art—was too small. In many of the questions of personal morality that had driven him to his original quest for objective probability, Keynes still saw himself as an "immoralist," but he had come to the view that certain conventions were necessary to make possible the space and tolerance for what he called "personal liberty" and the "diversification of . . . fancy." Thus, it is not surprising to find Keynes concluding *The General Theory* with a defense of his policy proposals against the libertarians who might object that the proposals will lead to more state control of individual lives.

Whilst, therefore, the enlargement of the functions of government, involved in the task of adjusting to one another the propensity to

---

34. If Patinkin (1983; 1990) is correct to argue that Keynes was not an advocate of the modern concept of rules following, he is clearly wrong to overlook the degree to which Keynes was nonetheless an advocate for a different type of rules (i.e., long-run stable policies) meant to foster stable social conventions.

consume and the inducement to invest, would seem to a nineteenth-century publicist or to a contemporary American financier to be a terrific encroachment on individualism, I defend it, on the contrary, both as the only practicable means of avoiding the destruction of existing economic forms in their entirety and as the condition of the successful functioning of individual initiative.[35]

Keynes's realization that there were many reasons for people to object to his ideas undoubtedly led him to the conclusion that their successful implementation would require "skill and guile." But while we can rightly wonder if his use of "guile" is not a bit of playful hyperbole, he no doubt saw the very real and delicate parameters of the problem of achieving his desired end. A nice example of this occurs in a well-known letter he wrote to Friedrich Hayek in 1944 to congratulate him on his new book, *The Road to Serfdom*. After beginning by telling Hayek that "morally and philosophically I find myself in agreement with virtually the whole of it; and not only in agreement with it, but in deeply moved agreement," Keynes goes on to discuss his practical disagreements with the book. In the process, he reveals the odd assortment of motivations and visions that lie behind opposition to and support for his own proposals.

I should therefore conclude your theme rather differently. I should say that what we want is not no planning, or even less planning, indeed I should say that we almost certainly want more. But the planning should take place in a community in which as many people as possible, both leaders and followers, wholly share your own moral position. Moderate planning will be safe if those carrying it out are rightly oriented in their own minds and hearts to the moral issue. This is in fact already true of some of them. But the curse is that there is also an important section who could almost be said to want planning not in order to enjoy its fruits but because morally they hold ideas exactly the opposite of yours, and wish to serve not God but the devil. Reading the *New Statesman & Nation* one sometimes feels that those who write there, while they cannot safely oppose moderate planning, are really hoping in their hearts that it will not succeed; and so prejudice more violent action. They fear that if moderate measures are sufficiently successful, this will allow a reaction in what you think the right and they think the

---

35. *JMK*, vii, 380.

wrong moral direction. Perhaps I do them an injustice; but perhaps I do not.[36]

Thus we find Keynes during the last ten years of life, as always, pushing with unmatched skill for the schemes and proposals he believed necessary for the solution to the economic problem. There were constant changes and innumerable compromises, but he never lost sight of his goal. In the context of the present story, he devised schemes to assuage business confidence and address the objections of Treasury mandarins, but he never lost hope that *something* could be done.[37]

Keynes's Uncertain Revolution

When we speak of the Keynesian Revolution, we might mean either the *theoretical* revolution he wrought in macroeconomics or the revolution in *economic policy* that occurred after the Great Depression. I have tried to argue that each of these revolutions involves uncertainty.

Keynes clearly made a conscious effort to introduce uncertainty to his theoretical revolution. While this effort may seem simplistic or unsophisticated by contemporary standards, it was an honest effort at theoretical innovation. In part, of course, economics was not as analytically sophisticated then as it is now; but, as I have tried to show, this also reflected Keynes's view that the technical apparatus for representing expectations was often only a heuristic and that there was a real risk that the heuristic would be reified. Although he might have made a more sophisticated model of expectations, he purposefully used a model that would allow him to discuss how business confidence and uncertainty about the future could change (with swings in confidence) and so affect interest rates, output, and employment.

Fully recovering this dimension of the Keynesian Revolution has been a difficult process. As Jacob Viner wryly noted, "In the history of economic thought, the highest honor that we can bestow upon our heroes is that they agree with us."[38] Thus, while the questions of Keynes's theoretical concern with uncertainty has been discussed since 1961, the discussion has most often led to the conclusion that Keynes is an ally of

---

36. *JMK,* xxvii, 387.
37. Dimand and Dimand 1990 contains an excellent explanation of Keynes's proposals (after *The General Theory*) to stabilize commodity prices using buffer stocks.
38. Viner 1972, 81.

some contemporary school of thought: Austrian, Post-Keynesian, Rational Expectationist. The discussion has also led to arguments that uncertainty is not integral to *The General Theory* at all; apparently people have become so concerned that Keynes might have been an adherent of one of these schools that it seemed best to deny the grounds for the possible affinity.[39] Amidst all this hero worship, it has been hard to see the historical Keynes at work.

This inability, on the part of economists, to see Keynes in historical context, has in turn led them to overlook the possible external causes for his concern with uncertainty. Historians of economic thought are not prone to considering the external influences in their work, and work on Keynes has been no exception. The focus of most work on Keynes is so purely internal, or focused on the sequence of his formal models, that external influences rarely enter the picture.

Thus, fully recovering the Keynesian Revolution in economic policy has not been easy either. Many people in the last decade have noted Keynes's changed concern with activist fiscal policy after 1933, but no one has linked this to either his changed position on probability or his work on economic policy. The lack of a full background to the changing course of Keynes's policy prescriptions has undoubtedly lent to our uncertainty over just what Keynesian Revolution (in economic policy) he might have been trying to lead. It is hard, given the facts, to see Keynes as an advocate of activist fine tuning, and the more we find out about him the more we understand why this is the case.

Likewise, seeing Keynes in historical context makes it much easier to understand his many references to irrationality in his later writings. Although he had possessed a firm anchor for his conception of rationality early in his life because of his ardent Platonism, later in his life he had lost this mooring. This left him "protesting and praying" (in his words) for a point of view to which he could no longer subscribe.[40] Seen in this light, his statements on irrationality simply give expression to his frustration that people would not act in the ways that he believed would make a better world (e.g., raise the level of employment). The inability to see Keynes in historical context has led to unnecessary efforts to give a rigid, theoretically based sense to his frustration.[41]

---

39. In addition to neoclassical arguments that Keynes had no theoretical interest in uncertainty, the neo-Ricardians have also argued against such an interpretation. See, for instance, Milgate 1983 and Magnani 1983.
40. This quotation comes from "My Early Beliefs." See chapter 1.
41. See, for instance, Lawson 1991 and O'Donnell 1989.

These quandries over rationality and das Maynard Keynes problem are much more easily understood in historical relief than they are as problems in contemporary economic theory.

But what is to be gained from this knowledge? In terms of contemporary policy, the lessons are not altogether clear. In retrospect, it seems that Keynes was wise to capitulate to the argument that expectations make a difference in the success of economic policies. This insight forms a common link between Keynes and contemporary macroeconomists and seems to point to a real condition in modern capitalism. But it is an insight rather than a clear guideline for good policy. We still do not know when policy will *instill* confidence and when it will *shake* confidence. How policy makers build and maintain credibility is an unanswered question.[42] When Paul Volcker announced in 1979 that the Federal Reserve would begin targeting the money supply rather than interest rates, he gained tremendous credibility as an inflation fighter. After failing to meet these monetarist targets for several years, he still had enough credibility that inflation was not ignited when the Federal Reserve allowed the money supply to grow in the double digits (annually) between 1985 and 1987. His continued credibility is not easily explained.

Nor are the ideological lessons clear-cut. Those who oppose activist policy in favor of a rules-based approach can undoubtedly claim an affinity with Keynes's later position. But before they press their claim too far, they must recognize that Keynes never became an advocate of laissez-faire; he saw limits to short-run activist economic policy, but saw a clear need for stable long-run policies. They should also realize that his conclusions about the role of business confidence in a capitalist society can easily be used to score some clearly Marxist points regarding the legitimation of capitalism. What does it mean in a democracy if economic policy must always be tailored to fit the desires of one class? Is this truly democratic? Again, as in the case of credibility, there are important unanswered questions.

But perhaps it is in those unanswered questions that we begin to find the value in a full historical understanding of Keynes. To understand the way that his thought changed and evolved allows him to become much more valuable than he is as an Austrian, a Post-Keynesian, or a Rational Expectationist.[43] Economists have been slow (or reluctant) to address many of the questions that Keynes's work raises as they have striven to

---

42. See, for instance, Blackburn and Christensen 1989.
43. Or, needless to say, more valuable than he is as a neoclassicist or neo-Ricardian.

become more and more technically sophisticated. And in an awkward reflection of this growing technical sophistication, historians of economic thought have likewise narrowed their focus to internalist questions of model structure. In fact, their internal focus has become so intense that the most well-known historian of economic thought, George Stigler, has argued that their work is only valuable if explicated in the terms of contemporary theoretical debate.[44] But this narrowing of the historian's purview is antithetical to the open dialogue that defines science. Not only do we lose valuable ideas from the past, we also lose a sense of economists as people open to the full range of human experience.

In a time when the best economic theorists have called for a return to a richer conception of theory informed by fact and history, historians of economics do not need to be afraid to write more complete histories of the discipline. Focusing on the combinations of internal and external influences that have produced scientific progress in the past is necessary to help ensure further progress. Thus, the value in understanding Keynes's uncertain revolution may lie as much in the picture it gives us of the process of scientific discovery as it does in pointing to a particular model or particular policy as the pinnacle of his achievement.

---

44. See especially the essays reprinted in Stigler 1982.

Bibliography

Public Record Office

CAB 58/150-1 Economic Advisory Committee, committee of economists
PRO 30/69/456 MacDonald Papers

Other Archives

Henderson Papers, Nuffield College, Oxford
Keynes Papers, King's College, Cambridge
Moore Papers, University Library, Cambridge
Ramsey Papers, University of Pittsburgh

Primary Sources

Henderson, Hubert D. 1935. Do We want Public Works? Reprinted in *The Inter-war Years and Other Papers*. Edited by Henry Clay. Oxford: Oxford University Press, 1955.

Hicks, J. R. 1939. *Value and Capital*. Oxford: Clarendon Press.

HMSO. 1931. Committee on Finance and Industry, *Minutes of Evidence*, 2 vols.

Keynes, J. M. 1910. Great Britain's Foreign Investments. *Political Quarterly* (February):37–53; in *JMK*, xv, 44–59.

———. 1911. Review of *The Purchasing Power of Money: Its Determination and Relation to Credit, Interest and Crisis*, by Irving Fisher, *Economic Journal* 21:393–38; in *JMK*, xi, 375–81.

———. 1913. How Far Are Bankers Responsible for the Alternations of Crisis and Depression? In *JMK*, xiii, 2–14.

———. 1920. *The Economic Consequences of the Peace*. London: Macmillan; *JMK*, ii.

———. 1921a. *A Treatise on Probability*. London: Macmillan; *JMK*, viii.

———. 1921b. The Depression of Trade. (London) *Sunday Times*, 4 September; in *JMK*, xvii, 259–65.

———. 1922. The Consequences to Society of Changes in the Value of Money. *The Manchester Guardian Commercial* 5:321–38; in *JMK*, iv, 1–28.

———. 1923a. *A Tract on Monetary Reform*. London: Macmillan; *JMK*, iv.

————. 1923b. Currency Policy and Unemployment. *The Nation and Athenaeum* 33:611–12.

————. 1929. The Treasury Contribution to the White Paper. *The Nation and Athenaeum* 18 May; in *JMK*, xix, 819–24.

————. 1930. *A Treatise on Money.* Vol. 1, *The Pure Theory of Money;* Vol. 2, *The Applied Theory of Money.* London: Macmillan; *JMK*, v; vi.

————. 1931a. The Future of the World. *The Sunday Express,* 27 September; in *JMK*, ix, 245–49.

————. 1931b. Review of *Foundations of Mathematics,* by Frank Ramsey, *The New Statesman and Nation* 2:407; in *JMK*, x, 336–39.

————. 1932. A Note on the Long-term Rate of Interest in Relation to the Conversion Scheme. *Economic Journal* 42:415–23; in *JMK*, xxi, 114–25.

————. 1933a. A Monetary Theory of Production. In *Der Stand und die nächste Zunkunft der Konjunkturforschung: Festschrift für Arthur Spiethoff.* Munich: Duncker and Humbolt; in *JMK*, xiii, 408–11.

————. 1933b. *The Means to Prosperity.* London: Macmillan; in *JMK*, ix, 335–56.

————. 1936. *The General Theory of Employment, Interest and Money.* London: Macmillan; *JMK*, vii.

————. 1937a. The General Theory of Employment. *Quarterly Journal of Economics* 51:209–23; in *JMK*, xiv, 109–23.

————. 1937b. How to Avoid a Slump. In *JMK*, xxi, 384–95.

————. 1940. *How to Pay for the War.* London: Macmillan; in *JMK*, ix, 367–439.

————. 1949. *Two Memoirs.* London: Rupert Hart-Davis; in *JMK*, x.

————. 1973a. *The General Theory and After: Part I, Preparation.* Edited by D. E. Moggridge; *JMK*, xiii.

————. 1973b. *The General Theory and After: Part II, Defense and Development.* Edited by D. E. Moggridge; *JMK*, xiv.

————. 1979. *The General Theory and After: A Supplement.* Edited by D. E. Moggridge; *JMK*, xxix.

————. 1981a. *Activities 1922–29.* 2 vols. Edited by D. E. Moggridge; *JMK*, xix.

————. 1981b. *Activities 1929–31.* Edited by D. E. Moggridge; *JMK*, xx.

————. 1982. *Activities 1931–39.* Edited by D. E. Moggridge; *JMK*, xxi.

Lavington, Frederick. 1922. *The Trade Cycle: An Account of the Causes Producing Rhythmical Changes in the Activity of Business.* London: P. S. King and Staples.

Marshall, Alfred. 1890. *The Principles of Economics.* London: Macmillan.

————. 1923. *Money, Credit, and Commerce.* London: Macmillan.

Marshall, Alfred, and Mary Paley Marshall. 1879. *The Economics of Industry.* London: Macmillan.

Moore, G. E. 1903. *Principia Ethica.* Cambridge: Cambridge University Press.

————. 1912. *Ethics.* Oxford: Oxford University Press.

Overstone, Lord. 1837. *Reflections Suggested by a Perusal of Mr. J. Horsky Palmer's Pamphlet on the Causes and Consequences of the Pressure on the Money Market.* London: Richardson.

Pigou, A. C. 1913. *Unemployment.* London: Williams and Norgate.

————. 1920. *Economics of Welfare.* London: Macmillan.

————. 1927. *Industrial Fluctuations.* London: Macmillan.

Ramsey, Frank P. 1922. Mr. Keynes on Probability. *The Cambridge Magazine* 11:1.

————. 1931. *Foundations of Mathematics.* London: Kegan Paul.

Secondary Sources

Arrow, Kenneth J. 1985. Maine and Texas. *American Economic Review* 75:320–23.

Baldwin, Thomas. 1984. Moore's Rejection of Idealism. In *Philosophy in History,* edited by Richard Rorty, J. B. Schneewind, and Quentin Skinner. Cambridge: Cambridge University Press.

————. 1988. Review of *Bloomsbury's Prophet: G .E. Moore and the Development of his Moral Philosophy,* by Tom Regan, *Mind* 97:129–33.

————. 1990. *G.E. Moore.* London: Routledge.

Barber, William J. 1990. Government as a Laboratory for Economic Learning in the Years of the Democratic Roosevelt. In *The State and Economic Knowledge,* edited by Mary O. Furner and Barry Supple. Cambridge: Cambridge University Press.

Bateman, Bradley W. 1987. Keynes's Changing Conception of Probability. *Economics and Philosophy* 3:97–119.

————. 1988. G. E. Moore and J. M. Keynes: A Missing Chapter in the History of the Expected Utility Model. *American Economic Review* 78:1098–1106.

————. 1990. Keynes, Induction, and Econometrics. *History of Political Economy* 22:359–79.

————.1991a. The Rules of the Road. In *Keynes and Philosophy,* edited by J. Davis and B. Bateman. Aldershot: Edward Elgar.

————. 1991b. Das Maynard Keynes Problem. *Cambridge Journal of Economics* 15:101–11.

————. 1991c. Hutchison, Keynes, and Empiricism. *Review of Social Economy* 49:20–36.

————. 1992. What We Do With Our Heroes. *Journal of Economic Perspectives* 6:204–6.

Baumol, William J. 1990. Sir John Versus the Hicksians, or Theorist Malgré Lui? *Journal of Economic Literature* 28:1708–15.

————. 1991. Toward a Newer Economics: The Future Lies Ahead! *Economic Journal* 101:1–8.

Bigg, Robert J. 1990. *Cambridge and the Monetary Theory of Production.* London: Macmillan.

Blackburn, Keith, and Michael Christensen. 1989. Monetary Policy and Policy Credibility. *Journal of Economic Literature* 27:1–45.

Brady, Michael E. 1993. J. M. Keynes's Theoretical Approach to Decision-making Under Conditions of Risk and Uncertainty. *British Journal of the Philosophy of Science* 44:357–76.

Carabelli, Anna. 1988. *On Keynes's Method.* London: Macmillan.

————. 1991. Comment on Keynes's Epistemology and Economic Methodology. In *Keynes as Philosopher-Economist,* edited by Roderick O'Donnell. London: Macmillan.

Clarke, Peter F. 1988. *The Keynesian Revolution in the Making.* Oxford: Oxford University Press.

————. 1990. The Treasury's Analytical Model of the British Economy between the Wars. In *The State and Economic Knowledge,* edited by Mary O. Furner and Barry Supple. Cambridge: Cambridge University Press.

Coddington, Alan. 1982. Deficient Foresight: A Troublesome Theme in Keynesian Economics. *American Economic Review* 72:480–87.

Colander, David. 1984. Was Keynes a Keynesian or a Lernerian? *Journal of Economic Literature* 22:1572–75.

Collard, David A. 1983. Pigou on Expectations and the Cycle. *The Economic Journal* 93:411–14.

Cottrell, Allin. 1993. Keynes's Theory of Probability and Its Relevance to His Economics: Three Theses. *Economics and Philosophy* 9:25–51.

Davidson, Paul. 1991. Is Probability Theory Relevant for Uncertainty? A Post-Keynesian Perspective. *Journal of Economic Literature* 5:129–43.

Davis, John B. 1989. Keynes on Atomism and Organism. *Economic Journal* 99:1159–72.

————. 1991a. Keynes's View of Economics as a Moral Science. In *Keynes and Philosophy,* edited by J. Davis and B. Bateman. Aldershot: Edward Elgar.

————. 1991b. Keynes's Critiques of Moore. *Cambridge Journal of Economics* 15:61–77.

Davis, J. Ronnie. 1971. *The New Economics and the Old Economists.* Ames: The Iowa State University Press.

Dimand, Robert W., and Mary Ann Dimand. 1990. J. M. Keynes on Buffer Stocks and Commodity Price Stabilization. *History of Political Economy* 22:113–24.

Dimsdale, N. H. 1981. British Monetary Policy and the Exchange Rate, 1920–1938. *Oxford Economic Papers.*

————. 1987. Keynes on British Budgetary Policy 1914–1946. In *Private Saving and Public Debt,* edited by Michael J. Boskin, John S. Flemming, and Stefano Gorini. Oxford: Basil Blackwell. 208–33.

Fitzgibbons, Athol. 1988. *Keynes's Vision.* Oxford: Oxford University Press.

Fussell, Paul. 1975. *The Great War and Modern Memory.* New York: Oxford University Press.

Gerrard, Bill. 1991. Keynes's *General Theory:* Interpreting the Interpretations. *Economic Journal* 101:276–87.

Gillies, Donald A. 1988. Keynes as a Methodologist. *British Journal of the Philosophy of Science* 39:117–29.

Gillies, Donald, and Grazia Ietto-Gillies. 1987. Probability and Economics in the Works of Bruno DeFinetti. *Economia Internazionale* 40:3–20.

———. 1991. Intersubjective Probability and Economics. *Review of Political Economy* 3:393–417.

Hansen, W. Lee. 1991. The Education and Training of Economics Doctorates: Major Findings of the American Economic Association's Committee on Graduate Education in Economics. *Journal of Economic Literature* 29: 1054–87.

Harcourt, Geoffrey C. 1987. Theoretical Methods and Unfinished Business. In *The Legacy of Keynes,* edited by David A. Reese. San Francisco: Harper & Row.

Harrod, Roy F. 1951. *The Life of John Maynard Keynes.* London: Macmillan.

Hirschman, Albert O. 1977. *The Passions and the Interests.* Princeton, N.J.: Princeton University Press.

Howson, Susan K., and Donald Winch. 1977. *The Economic Advisory Council, 1930–39.* Cambridge: Cambridge University Press.

Hutchison, T. W. 1953. *A Review of Economic Doctrines, 1870–1929.* Oxford: Clarendon Press.

———. 1968. *Economics and Economic Policy in Britain, 1946–1966.* London: George Allen and Unwin.

James, Harold. 1989. What is Keynesian About Deficit Financing? The Case of Interwar Germany. In *The Political Power of Economic Ideas: Keynesianism Across Nations,* edited by Peter A. Hall. Princeton, N.J.: Princeton University Press.

Kahn, Richard. 1984. *The Making of Keynes' General Theory.* Cambridge: Cambridge University Press.

Knight, Frank. 1921. *Risk, Uncertainty, and Profit.* New York: Houghton Mifflin.

Krueger, Anne O., Kenneth J. Arrow, Olivier J. Blanchard, Alan S. Blinder, Claudia Goldin, Edward E. Leamer, Robert Lucas, John Panzer, Rudolph Penner, T. Paul Schultz, Joseph Stiglitz, and Lawrence H. Summers. 1991. Report of the Commission on Graduate Education in Economics. *Journal of Economic Literature* 29:1035–53.

Kuttner, Robert. 1985. The Poverty of Economics. *The Atlantic Monthly* 255:74–84.

Laidler, David. 1991. *The Golden Age of the Quantity Theory.* Princeton, N.J.: Princeton University Press.

Lawlor, Michael. 1995. Keynes and Financial Market Processes in Historical Context. In *Higgling,* edited by Neil de Marchi and Mary Morgan. Durham, N.C.: Duke University Press.

Lawson, Tony. 1985. Uncertainty and Economic Analysis, *Economic Journal* 95:909–27.

———. 1991. Keynes and the Analysis of Rational Behaviour. In *Keynes as Philosopher-Economist,* edited by Roderick O'Donnell. London: Macmillan.

Levy, Paul. 1979. *Moore: G. E. Moore and the Cambridge Apostles.* London: Weidenfeld and Nicolson.

Littleboy, Bruce. 1990. *On Interpreting Keynes: A Study in Reconciliation.* London: Routledge.

McCloskey, Donald. 1988. Thick and Thin Methodologies in the History of Economic Thought. In *The Popperian Legacy in Economics*, edited by Neil De Marchi. Cambridge: Cambridge University Press.

Magnani, Marco. 1983. "Keynesian Fundamentalism": A Critique. In *Keynes's Economics and the Theory of Value and Distribution*, edited by John Eatwell and Murray Milgate. Oxford: Oxford University Press.

Matthews, R. C. O., C. H. Feinstein, and J. C. Odling-Smee. 1982. *British Economic Growth: 1856–1973*. Stanford: Stanford University Press.

Meltzer, Allan H. 1981. Keynes's *General Theory*: A Different Perspective. *Journal of Economic Literature* 19:34–64.

———. 1988. *Keynes's Monetary Theory: A Different Interpretation*. Cambridge: Cambridge University Press.

Middleton, Roger. 1985. *Towards the Managed Economy: Keynes, the Treasury and the Fiscal Policy Debate of the 1930s*. London: Methuen.

Milgate, Murray. 1982. *Capital and Employment: A Study of Keynes's Economics*. London: Academic Press.

———. 1983. Keynes on the "Classical" Theory of Interest. In *Keynes's Economics and the Theory of Value and Distribution*, edited by John Eatwell and Murray Milgate. Oxford: Oxford University Press.

Miron, Jeffrey A. 1991. The Role of Economic History in Economic Research. *Journal of Monetary Economics* 27:293–99.

Moggridge, Donald E. 1972. *British Monetary Policy, 1924–1931: The Norman Conquest of $4.86*. Cambridge: Cambridge University Press.

———. 1976. *Keynes*. London: Macmillan.

———. 1986. Keynes in Historical Perspective. *Eastern Economic Journal* 12:357–69.

———. 1992. *Maynard Keynes: An Economist's Biography*. London: Routledge.

Moggridge, Donald E., and Susan K. Howson. 1974. Keynes on Monetary Policy, 1910–46. *Oxford Economic Papers* 26:226–47.

O'Donnell, Roderick. 1989. *Keynes: Philosophy, Economics and Politics*. London: Macmillan.

———. 1991. Keynes on Probability, Expectations and Uncertainty. In *Keynes as Philosopher-Economist*, edited by Roderick O'Donnell. London: Macmillan.

Patinkin, Don. 1976. *Keynes' Monetary Thought*. Durham, N.C.: Duke University Press.

———. 1982. *Anticipations of the General Theory*. Chicago: University of Chicago Press.

———. 1983. New Perspectives or Old Pitfalls? Some Comments on Allan Meltzer's Interpretation of the *General Theory*. *Journal of Economics Literature* 21:47–51.

———. 1990. On Different Interpretations of the *General Theory*. *Journal of Monetary Economics* 26:205–43.

Peden, G. C. 1988. *Keynes, The Treasury, and British Economic Policy*. London: Macmillan.

Pollard, Sidney. 1994. New Light on an Old Master. *The Economic Journal* 104:138–53.

Popper, Karl. [1934] 1959. *The Logic of Scientific Discovery*. London: Hutchinson & Co. Originally published as *Logik der Forschung*, 1934.

Regan, Tom. 1986. *Bloomsbury's Prophet: G. E. Moore and the Development of His Moral Philosophy*. Philadelphia: Temple University Press.

Rooth, Tim. 1993. *British Protectionism and the International Economy: Overseas Commercial Policy in the 1930s*. Cambridge: Cambridge University Press.

Rotheim, Roy. 1981. Keynes's "Monetary Theory of Value" (1933). *Journal of Post Keynesian Economics* 3:568–85.

Runde, Jochen. 1990. Keynesian Uncertainty and the Weight of Arguments. *Economics and Philosophy* 6:275–92.

———. 1991. Keynesian Uncertainty and the Instability of Beliefs. *Review of Social Economy* 3:125–45.

———. 1994. Keynes after Ramsey: In Defense of *A Treatise on Probability*. *Studies in the History and Philosophy of Science* 25:97–121.

Russell, Bertrand. 1904. Review of *Principia Ethica*, by G. E. Moore, *Independent Review* 328–33.

Rymes, Thomas K., ed. 1989. *Keynes's Lectures, 1932–35*. Ann Arbor: University of Michigan Press.

Samuelson, Paul. 1946. Lord Keynes and the *General Theory*. *Econometrica* 14:187–200.

———. 1987. Out of the Closet: A Program for the Whig History of Economic Science. *History of Economics Society Bulletin* 9:51–60.

Schabas, Margaret. 1992. Breaking Away. *History of Political Economy* 24:187–203.

Schumpeter, Joseph. 1954. *A History of Economic Analysis*. Oxford: Oxford University Press.

Shackle, G. L. S. 1961. Recent Theories Concerning the Nature and Role of Interest. *Economic Journal* 71:421–36.

Skidelsky, Robert. 1967. *Politicians and the Slump: The Labour Government of 1929–31*. London: Macmillan.

———. 1985. *John Maynard Keynes*. Vol. 1, *Hopes Betrayed, 1883–1920*. London: Macmillan.

———. 1989. Keynes and the State. In *The Economic Borders of the State*, edited by Dieter Helm, Oxford: Basil Blackwell. 144–52.

———. 1992. *John Maynard Keynes*. Vol. 2, *The Economist as Savior, 1920–37*. London: Macmillan.

Solow, Robert M. 1985. Economic History and Economics. *American Economic Review* 75:328–31.

Stigler, George. 1965. Textual Exegesis as a Scientific Problem. *Economica* 32:447–50.

———. 1976a. Do Economists Matter? *Southern Economic Journal* 42:347–54.

———. 1976. The Scientific Uses of Scientific Biography with Special Reference to J. S. Mill. In *James and John Stuart Mill: Papers of the Centenary Confer-*

ence, edited by John Robson and Michael Laine. Toronto: University of Toronto Press.

————. 1982. *The Economist as Preacher, and Other Essays.* Chicago: University of Chicago Press.

Teichgraeber, Richard F. 1986. *"Free Trade" and Moral Philosophy: Rethinking the Sources of Adam Smith's Wealth of Nations.* Durham, N.C.: Duke University Press.

Tollison, Robert D. 1984. Adam Smith as a Regulator. *History of Economics Society Bulletin* 6:38–39.

Urmson, J. O. 1970. Moore's Utilitarianism. In *G. E. Moore: Essays in Retrospect,* edited by Alice Ambrose and Morris Lazerowitz. New York: Humanities Press.

Viner, Jacob. 1972. *The Role of Providence in the Social Order.* Princeton, N.J.: Princeton University Press.

Watt, D. E. 1989. Not Very Likely: A Reply to Ramsey. *British Journal of the Philosophy of Science* 40:221–27.

Weintraub, E. Roy. 1991. *Stabilizing Dynamics: Constructing Economic Knowledge.* Cambridge: Cambridge University Press.

Westall, Oliver M. 1992. *The Provincial Insurance Company, 1903–38: Family Markets, and Competitive Growth.* Manchester: Manchester University Press.

Williams, Bernard O. 1972. *Morality: An Introduction to Ethics.* New York: Harper & Row.

Winch, Donald. 1969. *Economics and Policy: A Historical Study.* New York: Walker and Company.

Winslow, E. G. 1986. "Human Logic" and Keynes's Economics. *Eastern Economic Journal* 12:413–30.

————. 1989. Organic Interdependence, Uncertainty, and Economic Analysis. *Economic Journal* 99:1173–81.

Wolfe, J. N. 1956. Marshall and the Trade Cycle. *Oxford Economic Papers* 8:90–101.

Index